THE ANTHEM BOOK.

THE

ANTHEM BOOK

OF THE

UNITED FREE CHURCH OF SCOTLAND
(1900-1929)

ISSUED BY AUTHORITY.

RECOMMENDED FOR USE BY THE SYNOD OF THE
PRESBYTERIAN CHURCH OF ENGLAND, 1909.

London : NOVELLO AND COMPANY, Limited.

MADE IN ENGLAND.

PREFACE.

AFTER the union of the Free and United Presbyterian Churches in 1900, a desire was expressed that a Book of Anthems should be prepared for use in the congregations of the United Church, and accordingly, in 1902, the General Assembly remitted to the Praise Committee "to prepare and issue an Anthem Book for use in congregations."

In carrying out this remit the Committee have judged it expedient to restrict the collection to anthems in the rendering of which the congregation, as well as the choir, may take part. They have endeavoured to provide an adequate supply of material suited to the needs of the many congregations of the church where it is desirable that the music employed should be of a somewhat simple nature; but they have also included compositions presenting greater degrees of difficulty to meet the requirements of congregations of higher musical attainments.

The anthems have been arranged according to their opening texts in the order of the books of Scripture, those with words not taken from Scripture being placed at the end; but for convenience in selection, a classified index has been added, in which the anthems are arranged according to topics.

The Committee desire to express their great indebtedness to the Sub-Committee by whom the book has been compiled, and specially to the Convener, Mr. William Cowan; they are also indebted to Mr. F. G. Edwards, London, for the care and attention bestowed by him on the preparation of the book for the press and the revision of the proofs, and to Dr. W. G. McNaught for similar services rendered in connection with the Sol-fa edition.

The collection is now issued by the Committee in the fervent hope that its use may stimulate devotion, and add variety and interest to the service of praise.

April, 1905.

ALPHABETICAL INDEX.

A*

INDEX OF SUBJECTS.

Will God in very deed.

1 Kings viii. 27—30; 2 Chronicles vi. 18—21.

J. Goss.

Will God in very deed dwell with men on the earth? Behold, the
heaven and heaven of heavens can-not contain Thee; how much less this
house which we have builded? Yet have Thou re-spect unto the prayer of Thy
servants, and to their sup-pli-ca-tion, O Lord, our God, to hearken unto the
cry and the prayer which Thy servants pray before Thee to-day: that Thine

WILL GOD IN VERY DEED.

eyes may be o·pen upon this house, upon this house night and day, that Thine

cres.   dim.

eyes may be o - pen upon this house . . night and day.

cres.   dim.

mf

Heark - en Thou to the sup - pli - ca-tion of Thy ser -vants.

mf

f   mf

Hear Thou from Thy dwelling-place, e - ven from heaven; and when Thou

f   mf

p   mf   p   pp

hear-est, for - give; when Thou hear·est, for - give, for - give.

p   mf   p   pp

O Lord, my God.

1 Kings viii. 28, 30.

C. MALAN.

Slowly.

O Lord, my God, O Lord, my God, hear Thou the prayer Thy ser-vant pray-eth; have Thou re-spect un - to his prayer, have Thou re-spect un - to his prayer. Hear Thou in heaven Thy dwelling-place, and when Thou hear-est, Lord, for - give: Hear Thou in heaven Thy dwelling - place, and when Thou hear-est, Lord, for - give, for - give, for - give, O Lord, for - give.

O Lord, my God.

1 Kings viii. 28, 30.

S. S. Wesley.

Larghetto.

O Lord, my God, O Lord, my God, hear Thou the prayer Thy

hear Thou the

cres.

ser - vant pray - eth, have Thou re-spect un - to his prayer, re -

prayer Thy servant pray - eth, have Thou re-spect, re -

dim.

- spect un - to his pray - er. Hear Thou in heaven Thy

dim.

- spect un - to his pray - er. Hear Thou in heaven Thy

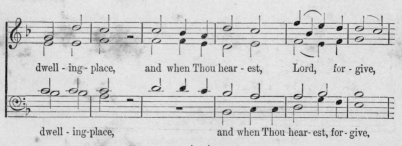

dwell - ing - place, and when Thou hear - est, Lord, for - give,

dwell - ing - place, and when Thou hear - est, for - give,

Hear Thou in heaven Thy dwell - ing - place, and when Thou hear - est,

Lord, for - give, and when Thou hear - est, Lord, for - give, for -

- give, . . for - give, . . and when Thou hear - est,

Lord, for - give, for - give, . . for - give, . . and when Thou

Lord, for - give, for - give, . . for - give, . .

hear - est, Lord, for - give. . . hear - est, Lord, for - give. . .

* This may be substituted for the foregoing three bars.

(5)

Thine, O Lord, is the greatness.

1 Chronicles xxix. 11.

J. KENT,
adapted by W. Shore.

Thine, O Lord, O Lord, is the great-ness, Thine, O

Lord, O Lord, is the great-ness, Thine, O Lord, O Lord, is the

great-ness, and the pow'r, and the glo-ry, and the

vic-to-ry, and the ma-jes-ty, the vic-to-ry, and

ma-jes-ty. Thine, O Lord, Thine, O Lord, is the

I will lay me down in peace.

Psalm iv. 8.

H. GADSBY.

Andante con moto. (♩ = 72.)

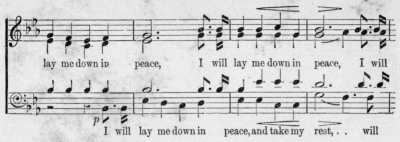

lay me down in peace, I will lay me down in peace, I will

I will lay me down in peace, and take my rest, .. will

lay me down in peace, in peace, . . and take my rest: ..

lay me down in peace, .. and take my rest: .. for it is

lay me down in peace, and take my rest: ..

Thou, Lord, on - ly, on - ly Thou that makest me dwell in

on - ly Thou that mak - est me

safe - ty, that makest me dwell in safe - ty, for it is Thou, Lord,

safe - ty, that makest me dwell in safe - ty, for

dwell .. in safe - - - - - ty, for

I WILL LAY ME DOWN IN PEACE.

6 I will lay me down in peace.

Psalm iv. 8.   W. H. GILL.

Quietly.

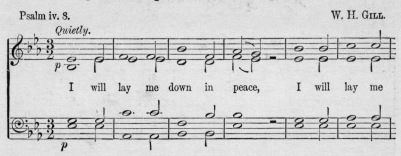

I will lay me down in peace, I will lay me

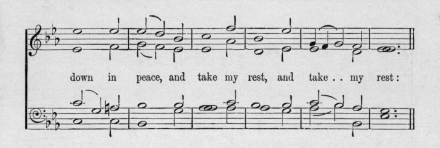

down in peace, and take my rest, and take .. my rest:

A little faster.

for it is Thou, Lord, on-ly, that mak-est me dwell in

safe-ty, for it is Thou, Lord, on-ly, that makest me dwell in

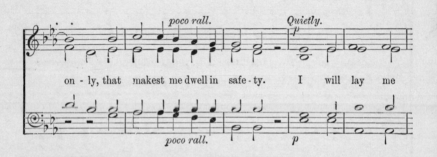

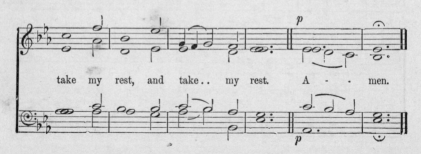

7
My voice shalt Thou hear in the morning, O Lord.

Psalm v. 3, 7.   J. Goss.

By permission of the Proprietors of *Congregational Church Music*,

Lead me, Lord.

Psalm v. 8 ; iv. 8.

S. S. Wesley.

lead me in Thy righteousness, make Thy way plain be - fore my

Solo. (Soprano.)

face For it is Thou, Lord, Thou, Lord, on - ly, that

cres. *dim.* *p* Chorus.

makest me dwell in . . safe - ty. For it is Thou, Lord,

cres. *dim.* *p* *rit.*

Thou, Lord, on - ly, that mak - est me dwell in . . safe - ty.

cres. *dim.* *p* *rit.*

(15)

The Lord will be a refuge.

Psalm ix. 9, 10.

G. J. Webb.

Moderato.

The Lord will be a ref - uge for the op - press - ed, a

ref - uge in times of trou - ble. And they that know, that

know Thy name will put their trust in Thee : .. for

Thou, Lord, hast not for - sa - ken them that seek ..

By permission of the Proprietors of *Congregational Church Music.*

Thee, . . for Thou, Lord, hast not for - sa - ken them, for - sa - ken

them . . that seek . . Thee. The Lord will be a ref - uge

mf

for the op - press- ed, a ref - uge in times of trou - ble. And

f

they that know, that know Thy name will put their

trust in Thee, . . will put . . their trust in Thee. . .

Let the words of my mouth.

Psalm xix. 14.

C. H. Perrot.

From *The Bristol Anthem Book*, by permission of Mr. W. Crofton Hemmons, Bristol

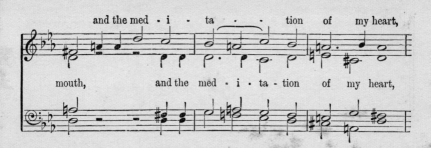

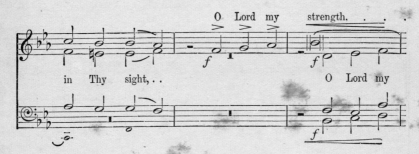

My God, look upon me.

Psalm xxii. 1—3.

J. Reynolds.

Moderato.

My God, my God, look up-on me, look up-on me:

why hast Thou for-sa-ken me, why hast Thou for-sa-ken me,

and art so far from my health, and from the words of

and art so far from my health, and from the words of my . . com-

and from the

health, and from the words of my com-

my . . complaint, the words of my com-plaint, and from the

- plaint, the words of my com-plaint, and from the words of

words of my complaint, the words of my com-plaint,

- plaint, the words of my com-plaint, and from the words of

words of my . . complaint, the words of my . . com-plaint?

my . . com-plaint, . . the words of my com-plaint?

and from the words of my complaint, the words of my com-plaint?

my complaint, the words of my complaint, of my com-plaint?

not; and in the night sea - son al - so I take no

not; and in the night sea - son al - so I . take no

rest, no rest, I take no rest, al - so I

rest, I take no rest, no rest, al - so I

take, I take no rest, I take no rest,

take, I take no rest, no rest, I

no rest, al - so I take, I take no rest.

take no rest, al - so I take, I take no rest.

CHORUS. *Moderato.*

But Thou con - tin - u - est ho - ly, O Thou wor - ship of Is - ra -

- el, Thou con - tin - u - est ho - ly, O . . Thou wor - ship of

slower.

Is - ra - el, O . . Thou wor - ship of Is - ra - el.

slower.

The Lord is my Shepherd.

Psalm xxiii. 1—4, 6.

G. A. MACFARREN.

right-eous-ness for His name's . . sake, . . His name's . . sake.

for His name's . . sake, . . His name's . . sake.

Yea, though I walk through the val-ley of the shad-ow of death,

Yea, though I walk through the val-ley of the shad - - - ow of death,

of the shad-ow of death,

yea, though I walk through the val - ley of the shad - ow of death,

yea, though I walk through the val - ley of the shad-ow of death,

I will fear no e - vil: for Thou art with me; Thy rod and Thy

I will fear no e - vil: for Thou . . art with me;

staff, Thy rod . . and Thy staff, Thy rod . . and Thy staff . . they

com - fort me, they com - fort me. Sure - ly, sure - ly

good - ness and mer - cy shall fol - low me.. all the

days of my life: and I will dwell in the house of the

Lord.. for ev - er, I will dwell in the house of the Lord.. for

ev - er, for ev - er, for.. ev - - - er.

for ev - - - er.

13   The Lord is my Shepherd.

Psalm xxiii.

W. Griffith.

Andante espressivo.

The Lord is my shep-herd; I shall not want, I shall not, I shall not want. He maketh me to lie down in green . . pas-tures: He leadeth me be-side the still wa - ters. He re-stor-eth my soul: He leadeth me in the paths of right-eous-ness, for His name's . . sake.

Bass Solo, or all the Basses.

Yea, though I walk through the valley of the shad-ow of death, I will fear no e - vil : for Thou art with me ; Thy rod and Thy staff they com - fort me. Thou pre - par - est a ta - ble be - fore me in the presence of mine en - e - mies : Thou a - nointest my

head with oil; my cup run-neth o - - - - ver.

CHORUS.

mf Sure · ly good-ness, good-ness and mer-cy shall fol-low me

all the days of my life: and I will dwell in the house of the

Lord, in the house of the Lord for ev - - er, in the

The earth is the Lord's.

Psalm xxiv. 1—5.

W. H. MONK.

The earth is the Lord's, and all that therein is, the compass of the world, and they that dwell there-in. For He hath founded it up-on the seas, and pre-par-ed it up-on the floods, pre-par-ed it up-on .. the floods. Who shall as-cend in-to the hill of the Lord, or who shall rise up in His ho-ly place? E-ven he,

e - ven he that hath clean . . hands, and a pure . . heart, and that hath not

lift up his mind un - to van - i - ty, nor sworn to de - ceive his

neigh - bour. He, he shall re - ceive the blessing from the Lord, and righteous -

- ness from the God of his sal - va - tion, the God of his sal -

- va - - tion. A - - - - - - - - men.

Shew me Thy ways, O Lord.

Psalm xxv. 4, 5.

J. LAMB.

Prayerfully.

Shew me Thy ways, O Lord; teach me Thy paths, shew me Thy ways, O Lord; teach me Thy paths. Lead me in Thy truth, and teach me, teach me, lead me in Thy truth, and teach me, teach me, for Thou art the God of my sal - va - tion, the God of my sal - va - tion; on Thee do I wait all the day, all the day.

16   One thing have I desired of the Lord.

Psalm xxvii. 4.

G. A. MACFARREN.

One thing have I de-sir-ed of the Lord, One thing have I de-sir-ed of the Lord, af-ter that will I seek; that I may dwell in the house of the Lord all the days of my life, to be-hold the beauty of the Lord, . . and to en-quire in His tem-ple, to be-hold the beauty of the Lord, . . and to en-quire in His tem-ple.

Sing unto the Lord.

17

Psalm xxx. 4, 5.

Joyfully.

E. PROUT.

f Sing unto the Lord, O ye saints of His, . Sing unto the Lord, O ye saints of His, . . and give thanks at the remembrance of His ho - liness. Sing unto the Lord, O ye saints of His, . . O ye saints, give O ye thanks, O ye saints, give thanks at the re-membrance of His ho - li-ness. saints, give thanks,

saints, give thanks,

A little slower.

mp For His anger en - dureth but a moment, His anger en -

Incline Thine ear.

Psalm xxxi. 2, 16.

F. H. Himmel.
Arranged by V. Novello.

Andante.

Shew Thy servant.

Psalm xxxi. 16, 17.

J. E. WEST.

Moderato. (♩ = 112.)

O love the Lord.

Psalm xxxi. 23, 24.

A. S. Sullivan.

Smoothly, and not too slowly. (♩ = 80.)

O love the Lord, all ye .. His saints; for the Lord pre - serv - eth

and plenteous - ly .. re - ward - -
them that are faithful, and plenteous - ly .. re - ward - -
and plen - teous - ly .. re - wardeth the

eth the proud do - er, and plen - teous - ly .. re
eth the .. proud .. do - er, and plen - teous - ly re -
eth .. the proud do - er, and plen - teous - ly .. re -
proud .. do - er, re - ward - - - -

wardeth the proud .. do - - er,
ward - - eth .. the proud .. do - er,
ward - - - eth, and plen - teous - ly ..
re - wardeth the proud
eth, dim - in - u - en - do.

O LOVE THE LORD. [No. 20.

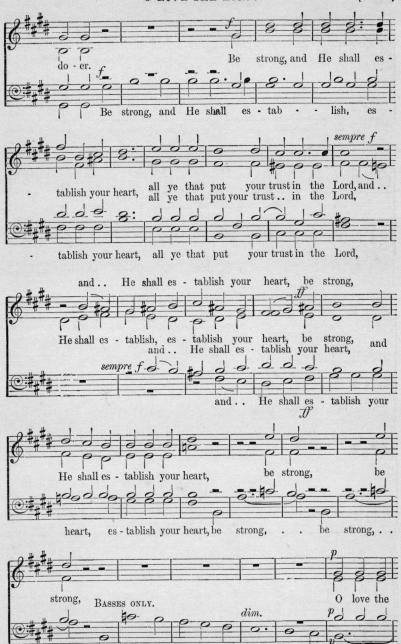

(43)

Rejoice in the Lord.

G. J. ELVEY.

Psalm xxxiii. 1, 2.

Allegro moderato.

Re - joice, re - joice, re - joice in the Lord, re -

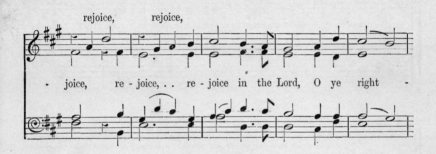

- joice, re - joice, .. re - joice in the Lord, O ye right -

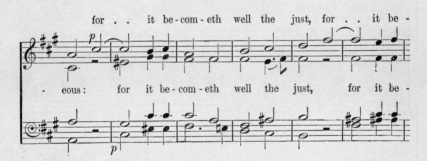

- eous: for it be - com - eth well the just, for it be -

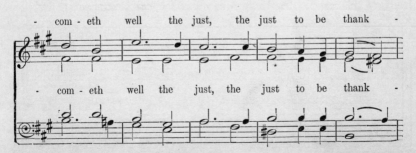

- com - eth well the just, the just to be thank -

ful. Praise the Lord with harp,   praise the Lord with harp :

Gt. Diaps.

Sw.

Sing   praises un - to Him, sing   praises un-to Him, sing

Sing   praises un - to Him,   sing   praises un - to

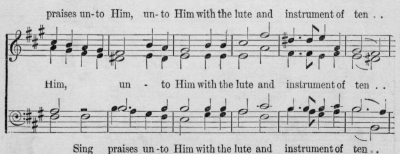

praises un-to Him, un- to Him with the lute and   instrument of ten . .

Him,   un - to Him with the lute and   instrument of ten . .

Sing   praises un-to Him with the lute and   instrument of ten . .

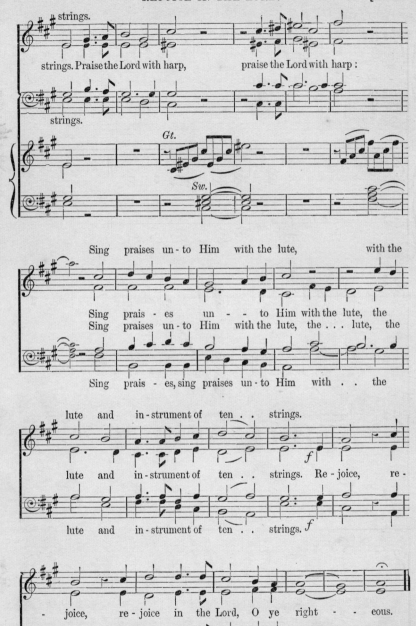

Rejoice in the Lord.

Psalm xxxiii. 1, 4, 5.

E. H. TURPIN.

Andante. Alla Breve.

O .. ye right - eous, O .. ye right - eous: for

O .. ye right - eous, .. O .. ye right - eous : ..

praise is come-ly for the up - right. For the word of the

Lord is right; and all His works are done in truth, for the

word of the Lord is right; and all His works are done in

truth, and all His works are done in truth. .. He

and all .. His works are done in truth, in truth.

Our soul waiteth for the Lord.

Psalm xxxiii. 20—22.

L. MASON.

Moderato.

mf

Our soul wait - eth for the Lord, our soul

wait - eth for the Lord; He is our help, is our

help and our shield; He is our help, is our help and our shield.

For our heart shall re - joice, . . re - joice . . in Him, our

heart shall re - joice . . in Him; be - cause we have trust - ed in His

ho - ly name, be - cause we have trusted in His ho - ly name.

Let Thy mer - cy, O Lord, be up - on us, ac - cording as we

hope, as we hope in Thee. Let Thy mer - cy, O

Lord, be up - on us, ac - cord - ing as we hope, as we hope in Thee.

24

O taste and see.

Psalm xxxiv. 8—10.

Andante, e con espressione. (♩ = 112.)

QUARTET, OR SEMI-CHORUS.

J. GOSS.

O TASTE AND SEE.

25 Blessed is he that considereth the poor.

Psalm xli. 1.

Moderato.

H. P. MAIN.

Blessed is he that con-sid-er-eth the poor, Blessed is

he that con-sid-er-eth the poor: the Lord will de-liv-er him in

time of trouble, the Lord will de-liv-er him in time .. of

trou-ble, the Lord will de-liv-er him, the Lord will de-liv-er him in

time .. of trou-ble, in time .. of .. trouble.

Blessed be the man.

Psalm xli. 1.

C. STEGGALL.

Moderato. (♩ = 92.)

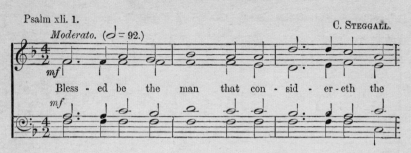

Bless - ed be the man that con - sid - er - eth the

poor .. and ... need - y, Bless - ed be the

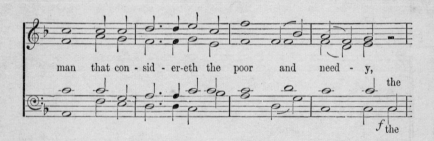

man that con - sid - er-eth the poor and need - y, the

the Lord shall . . . de - liv - er

the Lord shall de - liv - er him in ..

Lord shall de - liv - er him ... in .. the ... time, ... in ..

Lord shall ... de - liv - er him in the..

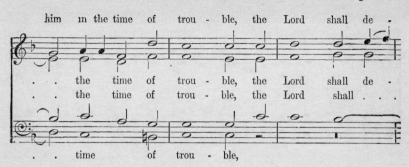

him in the time of trou - ble, the Lord shall de -

. . the time of trou - ble, the Lord shall de -
. . the time of trou - ble, the Lord shall . . .

. . time of trou - ble,

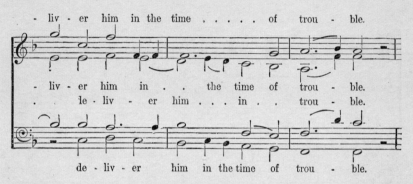

- liv - er him in the time . . . . . of trou - ble.

- liv - er him in . . the time of trou - ble.
. le - liv - er him . . . in . . trou - ble.

de - liv - er him in the time of trou - ble.

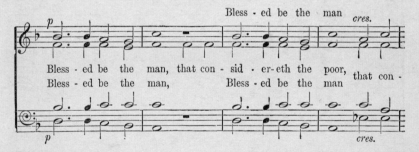

Bless - ed be the man

Bless - ed be the man, that con - sid - er - eth the poor,
Bless - ed be the man, Bless - ed be the man that con -

- sid - er - eth the poor . . and need - - y.

Like as the hart.

Psalm xlii. 1, 5.

Slowly. QUARTET, OR SEMI-CHORUS.

V. NOVELLO.

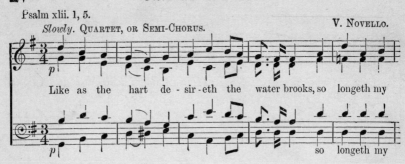

Like as the hart de - sir -eth the water brooks, so longeth my

so longeth my

CHORUS.

soul af - ter Thee, .. O God. Like as the hart de -

soul af - ter Thee, O God.

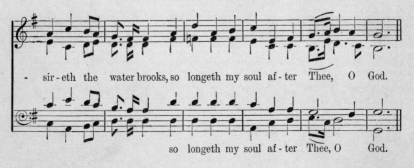

- sir -eth the water brooks, so longeth my soul af - ter Thee, O God.

so longeth my soul af - ter Thee, O God.

QUARTET, OR SEMI-CHORUS.

Why art thou so full of heaviness, so full . . . of

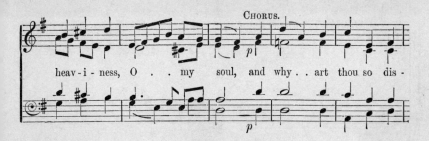

heav - i - ness, O . . my soul, and why . . art thou so dis -

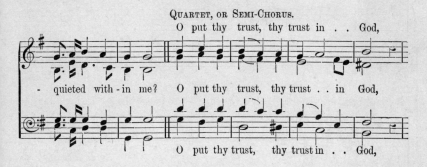

QUARTET, OR SEMI-CHORUS.

O put thy trust, thy trust in . . God,

- quieted with - in me? O put thy trust, thy trust . . in God,

O put thy trust, thy trust in . . God,

O put thy trust, thy trust in God, CHORUS.

O put thy trust, thy trust . . in God, O put thy trust, thy

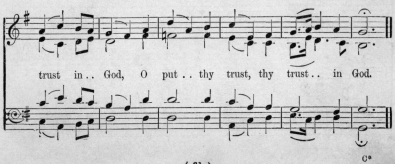

trust in . . God, O put . . thy trust, thy trust . . in God.

C*

Turn Thy face from my sins.

Psalm li. 9—11.

T. ATTWOOD.

Turn Thy face from my sins, . . and put out

all my mis - deeds. . . Make me a clean heart, O

God, . . and re - new a right spir - it with - in me, re -

Spir - it . . from me, Thy Ho - ly Spir - it . . from . . me.

CHORUS.

Cast me not a - way, . . a - way from Thy presence ; and

take not Thy Ho - ly Spir - it from me, and take not Thy Ho - ly

Spir - it from me, Thy Ho - ly Spir - it from . . me.

Turn Thy face from my sins.

Psalm li. 9—11.

A. S. Sullivan.

Andante espressivo.

Turn Thy face from my sins, and put out all my misdeeds.

Make me a clean heart, O God, and re - new a right spir - it with -

me, and take not Thy Ho - ly Spir - it   from   me.

Turn Thy face from my sins,   and put out all my misdeeds. Make me a

clean   heart, O   God,   and   re - new a right spir - it with -

30 Create in me a clean heart, O God.

Psalm li. 10—13.

E. Prout.

Cre - ate in me a clean heart, O God; and re - new a right

spir - it with - in . . me. Cast me not a - way from Thy presence; and

take not Thy Ho - ly Spirit from me, take not Thy Ho - ly Spirit

from me. Re - store un - to me the joy of Thy sal

Andantino.

- vation; and up - hold me, and up - hold me with Thy free spirit, and up -

- hold me with Thy free spirit. Then will I teach transgressors Thy

ways: and sinners shall be con - verted, and sinners shall be converted, con -

- verted unto Theé. Then will I teach transgressors Thy ways, and

sin - ners shall be con - vert - ed, con - vert - ed un - to Thee.

Psalm li. 17.   J. B. CALKIN.

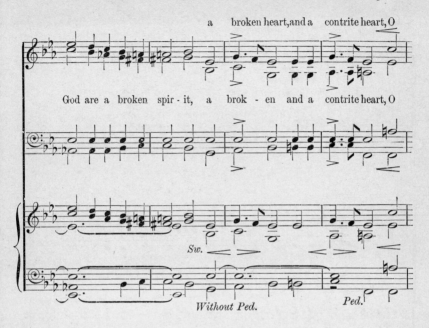

32 Cast thy burden on the Lord.

Psalm lv. 22.

W. B. BRADBURY.

Poco adagio.

Cast thy burden on the Lord, cast thy burden on the Lord, thy burden on the Lord, cast thy burden on the Lord, and

cres.

He shall sustain thee, and strengthen thee, and comfort thee,

mf *dim.* *mf*

He shall sustain thee, and comfort thee, He shall sus-

- tain thee, and com - fort thee, He shall sus - tain thee,

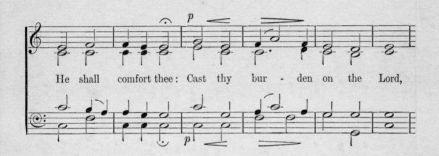

He shall comfort thee: Cast thy bur - den on the Lord,

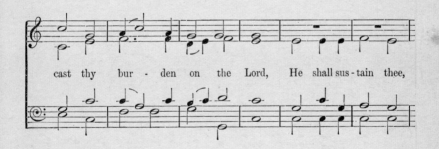

cast thy bur - den on the Lord, He shall sus - tain thee,

He shall comfort thee: Cast thy bur - den on the Lord.

Psalms lv. 22; xvi. 8; cviii. 4; xxv. 3.

MENDELSSOHN.
From the oratorio of "Elijah."

Cast thy bur-den up-on the Lord,

pp sempre legato.

cres.

and He shall sus-tain .. thee; He nev-er will suf-fer the

cres.

He is at thy right hand.

right-eous to fall. He .. is at thy right hand. Thy

He is at thy right hand.

mer - cy, Lord, is great, and far a - bove the heavens. Let none be made a - sha - med that wait up - on . . Thee.

34 Praise waiteth for Thee, O God, in Sion.

Psalm lxv. 1, 11, 13 ; lxvi. 8.

J. Goss

Praise waiteth for Thee, O God, in Si-on: and un-to Thee shall the

vow, shall the vow be per-formed. Thou crownest the year with Thy

goodness, Thou crownest the year with Thy goodness; and Thy paths drop

fatness, Thy paths drop fatness. The pastures are cloth-ed with

flocks; the valleys al - so are cover'd o - ver with corn; they

they

shout for joy, ... they al - so sing, they

shout for joy, they al - so sing,

Quicker.

shout for joy, they al - so sing. O bless our God, ye

peo - ple, and make the voice of His praise to be heard: bless our

God, bless our God, and make the voice of His praise to be heard.

35 Praise waiteth for Thee, O God, in Sion.

Psalm lxv. 1, 2.

C. Darnton.

Praise waiteth for Thee, O God, in Sion, and unto Thee shall the vow be perform'd, praise waiteth for Thee, O God, in Sion,

and un-to Thee . . . shall the vow,
and un-to Thee, un-to Thee shall the vow,
and un-to Thee, . . to Thee shall the vow, the vow be per-form'd.
and un-to Thee . . . shall the vow,

ALL VOICES IN UNISON.

Slower.

O Thou that hear-est prayer, . . O Thou that hear-est

HARMONY.

prayer, . . un-to Thee, . . un-to Thee . . shall all flesh

From *The Bristol Anthem Book*, by permission of Mr. W. Crofton Hemmons, Bristol.

O Thou that hearest prayer.

Psalm lxv. 2.

T. Hastings.

Moderato.

O Thou that hearest prayer, O Thou that hearest prayer, unto Thee, unto Thee, unto Thee shall all flesh come; unto Thee, unto Thee shall all flesh come.

O Thou that hearest prayer, O Thou that hearest prayer, unto Thee, unto Thee shall all flesh come. O Thou that hearest prayer, unto Thee, .. unto Thee shall all flesh come, unto Thee shall all .. flesh .. come.

God be merciful unto us.

Psalm lxvii.   (DEUS MISEREATUR.)

E. Bunnett.

- mong all   nations. Let the people   praise Thee,   praise Thee, O

God : yea, let   all   the .. peo - ple .. praise   Thee.

O .. let the   na - tions re - joice and be   glad: for Thou shalt

judge, shalt judge the folk .. righteously, and gov - ern the

na - tions up - on .. earth. Let the people praise Thee, praise Thee, O

God; yea, let all .. the .. peo - ple .. praise Thee.

D

Glory be to the Father, and to . . . the Son, and to . . the

Ho - ly . . Ghost; As it was in the be - ginning, is now, and ev-er

shall be ; . . world without end. . . . A - - men.

God be merciful unto us.

(DEUS MISEREATUR.)

Psalm lxvii.

F. Tozer.

God be mer-ci-ful un-to us, and bless us, and shew us the light of His coun-te-nance, and be mer-ci-ful, be mer-ci-ful un-to us. That Thy way may be known up-on . . . earth, Thy sa-ving health a-mong all . . na-tions. Let the people praise Thee, O God; yea, let all the people

praise Thee, O let the nations rejoice and be glad, for Thou shalt

judge the folk righteous-ly, . . and govern the nations up-on earth. Let the

peo-ple praise Thee, O God; . . yea, let all the peo-ple praise Thee.

rall.

rall.

rall.

Holy Ghost; As it was in the be -

Holy Ghost; As it was in the be - gin - ning, is

- gin - ning, is now, and ev - er shall be, is now, and e - er

now, and ev - er shall be, is now, and ev - er shall be : world with-

shall be : world with - out ... end. A - men.

- out end, world with - out end. A - men.

* C may be sung instead of G.

39 Let the people praise Thee, O God.

Psalm lxvii. 5—7.

T. HASTINGS.

Let the people praise Thee, O . . God; let the people

praise Thee, O . . God; let the people praise Thee, let the people

praise Thee, let all, let all the peo - ple praise Thee.

Then shall the earth yield her increase, then shall the earth yield her

increase; and God, e - ven our own God, shall bless .. us.

God shall bless . . . us.

God shall bless us, God shall bless .. us; and

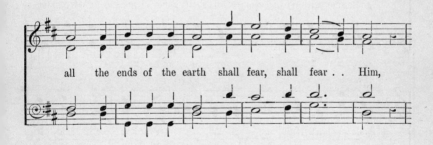

all the ends of the earth shall fear, shall fear .. Him,

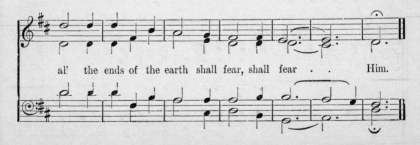

all the ends of the earth shall fear, shall fear . . Him.

D*

Thou shalt guide me.

Psalm lxxiii. 24—26.

J. BARNBY.

Moderato.

Thou shalt guide me, shalt guide me with Thy coun - sel, Thou shalt

guide me with Thy coun - sel, . . Thou shalt guide me, shalt

guide me with Thy coun - sel, shalt guide me, guide me,

guide me with Thy coun - sel, and af - terward re - ceive me to

glo - ry, and af - terward re - ceive me to glo - ry.

ALL VOICES IN UNISON.

Whom have I in heav'n but Thee, whom have I in heav'n but Thee? and there is none up-on earth, none up-on earth that I de - sire be - side Thee, none up-on earth, none up- on earth, there is none I de -

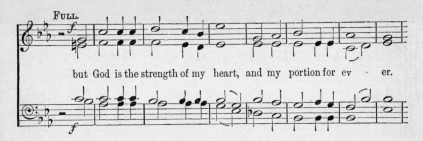

but God is the strength of my heart, and my portion for ev - er.

My flesh and my heart faileth, my flesh and my heart faileth:

but God is the strength of my heart, and my portion for

ev - er, . . my por - tion for ev - er, for ev - er.

41 O how amiable are Thy dwellings.

Psalm lxxxiv. 1—4.

C. Simper.

Andante.

Sopranos and Altos Full, or Solo Voices.

O how a - miable are .. Thy dwellings, O how a - miable

are .. Thy dwellings, Thou Lord . . . of hosts. . .

Chorus, or Quartet.

My soul longeth, yea, e - ven fainteth for the courts

of the Lord: .. my heart and my flesh cri - eth out for the

Psalm lxxxvi. 1, 6, 11, 12.

A. E. Grell.

Slowly.

Bow down Thine ear, bow down Thine ear, O Lord, hear me,

bow down Thine ear, O Lord, hear me, O Lord, hear me; for

I am poor, am poor and need-y, am poor and need-y. Give

ear, O Lord, un-to my prayer; and at-tend to the voice of my

sup - pli - ca - tions. Teach me Thy way, O Lord; I will walk in Thy

truth; u - nite my heart, u - nite my heart to fear Thy name.

Faster.

I will praise Thee, O Lord my God, with all my heart:

and I will glo - ri - fy Thy name, will glo - ri - fy Thy name for

for ev - - - er - - more. A - men.

ev - er - more, for ev - er, ev - er - more. A - men.

for ev - - - er - - more. A - men.

Comfort, O Lord, the soul of Thy servant.

Psalm lxxxvi. 4.

W. CROTCH.
Arranged by J. GOSS.

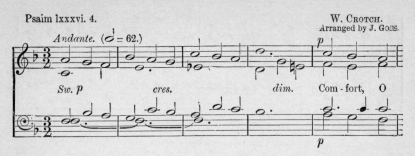

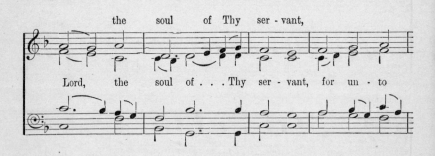

Thee do I lift up my soul: com - fort, O Lord, the

com-fort, O Lord, the

soul of Thy ser - vant, for un - to Thee do I . .

soul of Thy ser - vant,

lift up my soul, do I lift up my soul: com fort, O

Lord, . . the soul of Thy ser -vant, for un - to Thee do I . . .

lift up my soul, do I lift up my . . soul.

dim - in - u - en - do.

44 Whoso dwelleth under the defence.

Psalm xci. 1, 4.

W. Griffith.

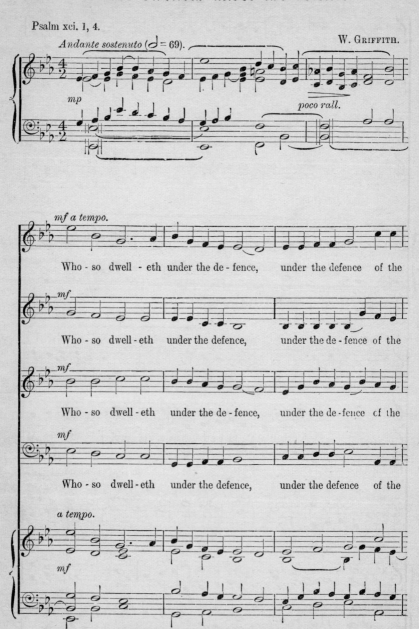

Who - so dwell - eth under the de - fence, under the defence of the

Who - so dwell - eth under the defence, under the de - fence of the

Who - so dwell - eth under the de - fence, under the de - fence of the

Who - so dwell - eth under the defence, under the defence of the

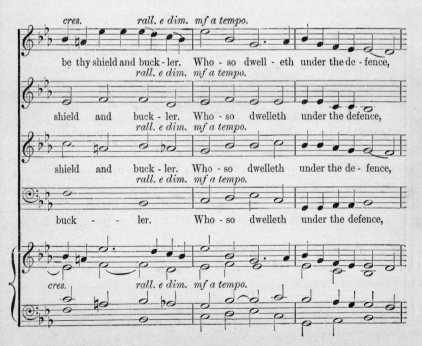

dim.
shad - ow of the Al - might - - - y.
dim.
might - y, the Al - might - - - y.
dim.
- - der the shad - ow of the Al-might - y.
dim.
the Al - might - - - - - - y.
dim.
mp
He shall defend thee under His wings, His faithfulness and truth shall
mp He shall de - fend . . thee under His wings, His
mp
He shall de - fend . . thee under His wings, His
mp
He shall de - fend thee under His wings, His faith- ful -
mp

under the defence of the most High, shall a-bide under the shadow, a-

under the defence of the most .. High, shall a - bide .. un - der the

under the defence of the most .. High, shall a - bide .. un - der the

under the defence of the most High, shall a - bide . . un - der the

- bide un - der the shad - ow . . of the Al - might - - y.

shad - - - ow . . of the Al - might - - y.

shad - - - ow . . of the Al - might - - y.

shad - ow, the shad - ow . . of the Al - might - - y.

45   O come, let us worship.

Psalm xcv. 6, 7.

R. HORNER.

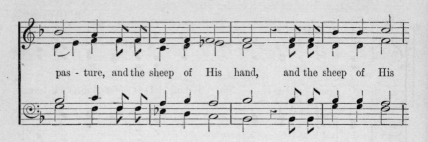

pas - ture, and the sheep of His hand,   and the sheep of His

hand.   O   come,   O   come,   let us   wor - ship and bow

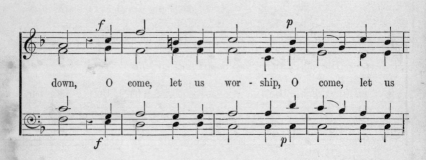

down,   O   come,   let us   wor - ship,   O   come,   let us

kneel,   O   come,   let us kneel be -fore the Lord our Mak - er.

Psalm xcvi. 6.

Quickly.

M. GREENE.

Honour and maj-es-ty are be-fore Him, honour and maj-es-ty

strength and

are be-fore Him: strength and beau-ty,
strength and beau-ty, beau-ty, strength and beauty are

strength and beau-ty, beauty are

beau-ty are in His sanctu-a-ry.

in .. His sanc-tu-a-ry. Honour and maj-es-ty are be-
in .. His .. sanctu-a-ry.

in His sanc-tu-a-ry.

strength and beauty are in .. His sanctu-a-ry,

-fore Him: strength and beau-ty, beau-ty are in .. His sanc-tu-a-ry,
strength and

strength and beau-ty,

strength and beauty are in .. His sanctu-a-ry.

strength and beau-ty, beauty are in .. His sanc-tu-a-ry. A-men.
strength and

strength and beau-ty,

Psalm xcvi. 9, 10.

T. Smith.

Moderato.

O worship the Lord in the beau-ty of ho-liness, wor-ship the Lord in the beauty of ho-liness: let the whole earth, let the whole earth, let the whole earth, let the whole earth standin awe of Him. Worship the Lord in the beau-ty of ho-liness, worship the Lord,

48   O worship the Lord.

Psalms xcvi. 9 ; lxviii. 4.

G. J. ELVEY.

awe of Him, let the whole earth stand in awe, stand in awe of

Him, let the whole earth stand in awe, in awe of Him. . .

(♩ = 84.)

O sing un-to God, sing praises to His name, and re-joice, re-

and re-joice, and re-

sing . . unto

- joice be-fore Him. O sing unto God, O sing unto God, sing . .

sing, sing,

- joice be-fore Him, O sing unto God, sing, sing,

God, sing . . unto God, sing . . unto God,

. . . unto God, sing . . unto God, unto God, sing praises to His

sing unto God,

sing, sing unto God, sing unto God,

49 O be joyful in the Lord.

(JUBILATE DEO.)

Psalm c.

S. S. Wesley.

(♩ = 108.)

O be joyful in the Lord, all ye lands: serve the Lord with gladness, and come before His presence . . with a song. Be ye sure that the Lord He . . is God: it is He that hath made us, and not we our- selves; we are His . . people, and the sheep of His pas - ture. O go your way in - to His gates with thanksgiv - ing, and in - to His courts with

praise: be thankful un-to Him, and speak good of His name.   For the Lord is

gracious, His mer-cy is ev-er-last-ing: and His truth en-dureth from

gen-er-a-tion to gen-er-a-tion. Glory be to the Father,

and to the Son, and to the Ho-ly Ghost; As it was in the be-

is now, and ever shall be: world with-out end. A-men.

-ginning, is .. now, and ev-er shall be: world with-out end. A-men.

O be joyful in the Lord.

(JUBILATE DEO.)

Psalm c.

G. M. GARRETT.

O be joyful in the Lord, all ye lands : serve the Lord with

gladness, and come before His presence with a song. Be ye

sure that the Lord He is God : . . it is He that hath made us,

and not we our - selves; we are His people, we are His people,

and the sheep of His pas - ture, and the sheep of His

pas - ture. O go your way into His gates with thanksgiving, and

Slowly, and with much firmness.

($\d$ = 60.)

in - to His courts, His courts with praise : be thank - ful .. un - to Him, be

thank - ful .. un - to Him, and speak good of His name.

cres.

For . the Lord, the Lord is .. gracious, His mer - cy is ev - er -

- last - ing: .... and His truth en - dur - eth, His truth en -

- dur - eth .. from gener - a - tion to gen - er - a - tion.

Sw.

dim.

Vivace.

Glo - ry be to the Fa - ther, and to the Son,

Vivace. (♩ = 132.)

E*

51

My song shall be of mercy and judgment.

Psalm ci. 1, 2.

Adapted from J. CLARK by L. MASON.

Moderato.

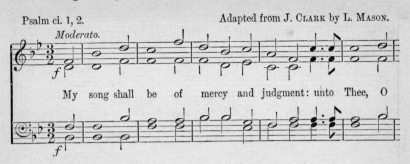

My song shall be of mercy and judgment: unto Thee, O

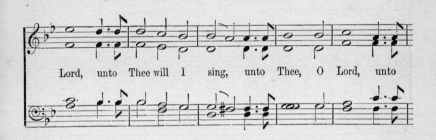

Lord, unto Thee will I sing, unto Thee, O Lord, unto

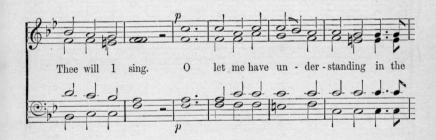

Thee will I sing. O let me have un - der - standing in the

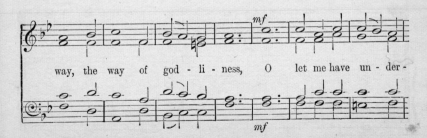

way, the way of god - li - ness, O let me have un - der -

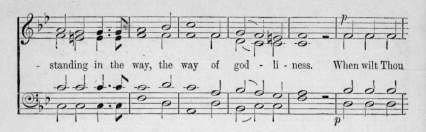

- standing in the way, the way of god - li - ness.   When wilt Thou

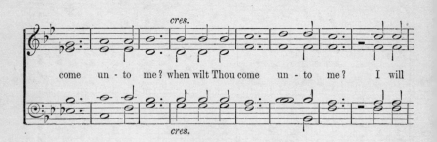

come un - to me? when wilt Thou come un - to me?   I will

walk in my house with a per - fect heart, I will walk in my house with a

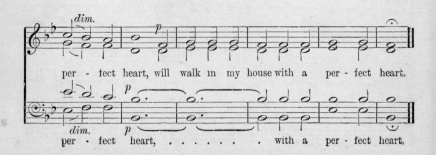

per - fect heart, will walk in my house with a per - fect heart.

per - fect heart, ... with a per - fect heart.

52

Bless the Lord, O my soul.

Psalm ciii. 1—3.

Brightly. (♩ = 104.)

E. J. HOPKINS.

Bless the Lord, .. O .. my soul: and all that is within me, bless His holy

name. Bless the Lord, .. O .. my soul, and for - get not, for - get not ..

and for-get not all .. His ben - e - fits:

all His bene - fits, and for - get not, and for-get not all His ben - e - fits;
all .. His ben-e - fits:

and for-get not all His ben - e - fits:

Smoothly.

Who for - giveth all thine in - i - quities; who healeth all, all thy dis -

- eas - es; who for - giv - eth all thine in - i - quities; who healeth all,

all thy dis - eas - es,   heal - eth all, . . all thy dis - eases.   Bless the

Lord, . . O . . my   soul : and all that is with - in me, bless His ho - ly

name, and all that is with - in me,   bless His ho - ly name, and all that is with -

- in me,   all that is with- in me,   bless,   bless His ho - ly   name,

bless,   bless His ho - ly name, His ho- ly, His ho - ly   name. . .

53

He watereth the hills.

Psalm civ. 13, 14, 24.

W. SPINNEY.

He wa-tereth the hills, the hills from a-bove; the earth is filled with the fruit of Thy works. He wa-tereth the hills, the hills from a-bove; the earth is filled with the fruit of Thy works. He bringeth forth

He bringeth forth grass for the

QUARTET. *Unaccompanied (if possible).*

HE WATERETH THE HILLS.

wis - dom hast Thou made them all : the earth, the earth is full, . . is

full . . of Thy riches. O Lord, how manifold

are Thy works! in wis - dom hast Thou made them all : the

earth is full, the earth is full, is full . . of Thy

rich - es. A - -

- men, A - - men. . .

Psalms civ. 24 ; lxv. 13 ; ciii. 2.   J. Barnby.

soul, and for - get not all . . His ben - e - fits. Praise the

Lord, O my soul, praise the Lord, O my soul, and for - get not

all . . His ben - e - fits. Praise the Lord, praise the Lord.

Remember me, O Lord.

Psalm cvi. 4, 5.

G. A. MACFARREN.

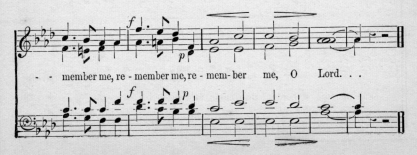

What shall I render.

Psalm cxvi. 12—14.

Slowly.

A. H. BROWN.

What shall I ren - der un - to the Lord for all His ben - e - fits to - ward . . me, for all His ben - e - fits to - ward . . me, to - ward . . me? I will take the cup of sal - va - tion, and call up-on the name of the Lord, and call up-on the name of the Lord, the name of the Lord. I will pay . . my I will

vows, I will pay . . my vows, my vows . . un-to the

pay . . my vows, will pay my vows . . un-to the

I will pay . . my vows, my vows . . un-to the

Lord, . . un-to the Lord . . . now in the presence of

all . . His peo-ple, now in the presence of all . . . His

peo-ple. Praise ye the Lord, . . praise ye the Lord, . . .

Alternative ending.

praise . . ye . . . the Lord . . . Lord. . .

57   O praise the Lord.

Psalm cxvii.

With spirit.

The Earl of WILTON.

O praise the Lord, O praise the Lord, all ye nations:

praise Him, all ye people, praise Him, all ye people, praise Him, O

praise Him, all . . ye peo - ple, praise Him, O praise Him,

QUARTET, OR SEMI-CHORUS. *Slower.*

all ye people. For His mer - ci - ful kindness is

ev - er . . more . . and more to - wards us: and the truth, the

truth of the Lord en - dur - eth for ev - er, en - dur - eth for

ev - er; His mer - ci - ful kindness is ev - er more and

and the truth of the Lord . . . . . en -

more to - wards us, and the truth of the

- dureth, en - dureth for ev - er,

Lord . . . . en - dureth, the truth of the Lord .. en -

and the truth of the Lord, the truth of the Lord en -

Slower. CHORUS. *With spirit.*

- dureth, en - dureth for ev - - er. O praise the Lord,

- dur - - eth for ev - - er. *f*

O PRAISE THE LORD.

O praise the Lord, all . . ye na - tions : praise Him, all ye

peo - ple, praise Him, all ye peo - ple, praise Him, O praise Him,

all ye peo - ple, praise Him, O praise Him, all ye

peo - ple. Praise the Lord, praise the Lord, praise the Lord, praise the Lord,

praise the Lord, praise the Lord, O praise the Lord. A - men.

O praise the Lord.

Psalm cxvii.

E. J. HOPKINS.

Spirited and bold. ($\dot{\bullet}$ = 116.)

O praise the Lord, all ye nations: praise Him, praise Him,

all .. ye people. O praise the Lord, all .. ye nations:

Quietly and a little slower. *

praise Him, praise Him, all ye peo-ple. For His merciful

kindness is great to-ward us: and the truth of the Lord en -

- dur-eth for ev-er, for His mer-ci-ful kindness is great to -

* This movement may be sung without Accompaniment.

na - tions: praise Him, praise Him, all . . ye peo - ple.

Praise ye the Lord. Praise ye the Lord. . . .

59 The Lord is my strength and my song.

Psalm cxviii. 14, 19, 22, 24.

W. H. MONK.

($\bullet$ = 96.)

The Lord is my strength, my strength and my song, and is . . be-

- come my sal - va - tion, and is . . become my sal - va - -

and is be - come, be - come my sal - va - tion.

- tion, and . . is be - come,

and is . . be - come, be - come my sal - va - tion.

be - come my . . . . sal - va - tion.

THE LORD IS MY STRENGTH AND MY SONG.

cor - ner, is be - come the head-stone in the cor - - ner.

This is the day which the Lord hath made; we . . . will re -

- joice and be glad in it, we will re - joice and be

we will re - joice . . . . . and be

glad in it, we . . will re - joice . . . . and be
we will re - joice . . . . . and be
we will re - joice . . . . . and be

glad in it. *Slower.*

glad in it. Hal - le - lu - jah. A - - men.

glad in it. *Slower.*

60 This is the day which the Lord hath made.

Psalm cxviii. 24; 1 Corinthians xv. 20—22, 57.

J. SEWELL.

This is the day which the Lord hath made;

we will re- joice, . . . we will rejoice and be glad in it. *1st time.*

we will rejoice, we will rejoice and be glad in it.

it. *2nd time.* it. For now is Christ risen, for now is Christ risen from the

dead, and become the first fruits .. of them that slept.

For since by man came death, by man came al - so the resurrection

of the dead. For as in Adam all die, e'en so in

Christ shall all be made a - live. Thanks be to God, which giveth us the

vic - to-ry, thanks be to God, which giveth us the vic - to ry

through our Lord Je - sus Christ, through our Lord Je - sus Christ. Thanks be to

Thanks be to God, which giv - eth us the vic - to - ry,

God, ...

ff Thanks be to God,

Thanks be to God, which giveth us the victory through our Lord

Jesus Christ... Hallelujah! Amen.

61 Teach me, O Lord.

Psalm cxix. 33.

T. Attwood.

Quietly.

teach me, teach me the

Teach me, O Lord, the way of Thy statutes, teach me, teach me
teach me, teach me

way of Thy statutes;

the way of Thy statutes; and I .. shall keep it, and I .. shall

the way of Thy statutes;

and

keep .. it unto the end, and I shall keep it, and

and I shall keep it,

Teach me, O Lord.

Psalm cxix. 33, 34.

Moderato.

G. W. MARTIN.

Teach me, O Lord, the way of Thy statutes; and I shall keep it un-

-to the end, and I shall keep it un-to . . the end, Teach me, O

Lord, the way of Thy statutes; and I . . shall keep it un-to the end, and

I . . shall keep it un-to the end. Give me under-standing, and

I shall keep Thy law; yea, I shall keep it with my whole heart.

63   ## I will lift up mine eyes.

Psalm cxxi. 1, 2, 5—8.

Moderato.

J. CLARKE-WHITFELD.

I will lift up mine eyes unto the hills, from whence cometh my help, I will lift up mine eyes unto the hills, from whence com - eth my help. My help cometh even from the Lord, my help cometh even from the Lord, who hath made heav'n and earth, who hath made heav'n and earth.

BASS SOLO.

The Lord Himself is thy keeper, the Lord Himself is thy

Andante largo.

CHORUS. *Brightly.*

The Lord shall preserve thee from all e - vil; yea, it is He that shall keep thy soul. The Lord shall preserve thy go-ing out, thy go-ing out and coming in, from this time forth, for ev - ermore. The Lord shall preserve thee yea, it is He that shall keep thy soul: Hal - le - lu - - jah, A - - - - men.

from all e - vil; yea, it is He that shall keep thy soul: from this time forth, for ev - ermore, from this time forth, for ev - ermore. A - - men.

yea, it is He that shall keep thy soul: A - - - - men, A - - - men.

Psalm cxxii. 6, 7.

L. MASON.

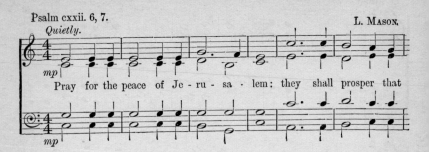

Pray for the peace of Je-ru-sa-lem: they shall prosper that

love . . . thee. Peace be with-in thy

Peace be with-in, with-in thy

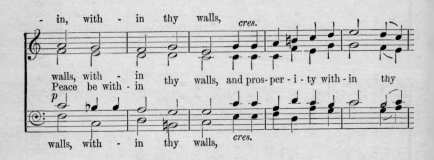

-in, with-in thy walls, walls, with-in thy walls, and pros-per-i-ty with-in thy

Peace be with-in thy walls, walls, with-in thy walls,

pal-a-ces. -ces. Hal-le-lu-jah, Hal-le-lu-jah! Hal-le-lu-jah!

Search me, O God.

Psalm cxxxix. 23, 24.

L. Mason.

Prayerfully.

Search me, O God, and know .. my heart: try me, and know my thoughts: and see if there be an - y wick - ed way in me, and lead me in the way, .. in the way ev - er - last - ing, and lead me in the way, .. in the way ev - er - last - ing. A - men.

cres. sempre.

66 Enter not into judgment.

Psalm cxliii. 2

J. Goss.

(164)

Enter not into judgment.

Psalm cxliii. 2.

T. Attwood.

Enter not into judg - ment with Thy servant, O Lord; for in Thy sight shall no man liv - ing be just - i - fied. En - ter not in - to judg - ment with Thy servant, O Lord; for in Thy sight shall no man

The eyes of all wait on Thee.

Psalm cxlv. 15, 16.

G. J. ELVEY.

The eyes of all wait on Thee, .. O Lord, and Thou givest them their meat in due sea - son. The eyes of all wait on Thee, .. O Lord, and Thou givest them their

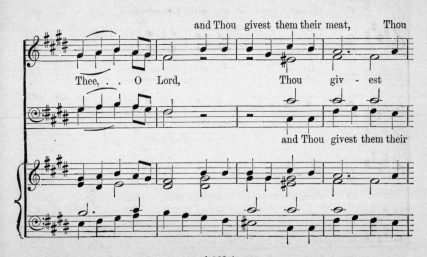

THE EYES OF ALL WAIT ON THEE.

69   **Remember now thy Creator.**

Ecclesiastes xii. 1.

E. Prout.

Remember now Thy Cre-a-tor in the days of thy youth, re-member now, . . . re-member now, . . . re-member now thy Cre-a-tor, re-mem-ber now thy Cre-a-tor in the days of thy youth, while the e-vil days come not, while the e-vil days come not, nor the years draw nigh, where-in thou shalt say, I have no pleasure

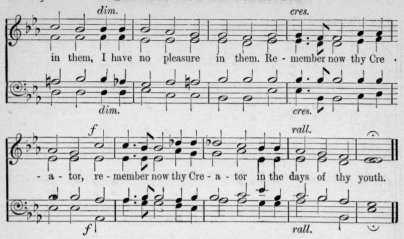

in them, I have no pleasure in them. Re - member now thy Cre - a - tor, re - member now thy Cre - a - tor in the days of thy youth.

70   Remember now thy Creator.*

Ecclesiastes xii. 1, 14.

W. GRIFFITH.

Moderato. (♩ = 88.)

Re - member now thy Cre - a - tor in the days of thy youth, . . re - member now thy Cre - a - tor in the days of thy
in the days . . of thy
in the days of thy

* The first movement may be used as a separate anthem, ending at the double bar on *p.* 174.

Copyright, 1899, *by W. Griffith.*

-mem - ber now thy Cre - a - tor in the days of thy . .

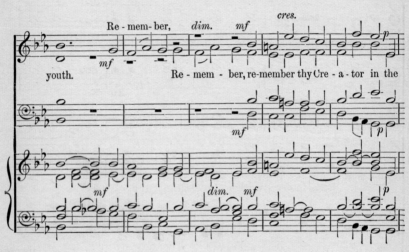

youth. Re - mem - ber, re-member thy Cre - a - tor in the

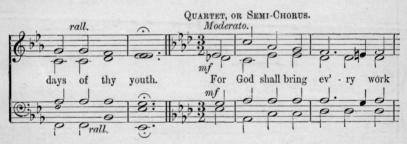

QUARTET, OR SEMI-CHORUS.
Moderato.

days of thy youth. For God shall bring ev' - ry work

in - to judgment with ev' - ry, ev' - ry se - cret thing.

REMEMBER NOW THY CREATOR.

71   Behold, a Virgin shall conceive.

Isaiah vii. 14 ; ix. 6.

T. SMITH.

Rather quickly.

Be - hold, a virgin shall conceive, and bear a Son, and shall call His name Im - man - u - el, God with us.

Allegro.

For unto us a Child is born, for unto us a Son is given, for unto us a Child is .. born, for unto us a Son is given, and His name shall be call - ed Won - der - ful, Coun - sel - lor, The

72 The Lord God will wipe away tears.

Isaiah xxv. 8.

J. V. ROBERTS.

Andante.

The Lord God will wipe a - way tears from off all fac - es, the

Lord God will wipe a - way tears from off all fac - es, the Lord God, the

Lord God will wipe a - way tears, wipe away tears from off all

peo - ple shall He take a - way; for the Lord hath spoken it, the

Lord hath spoken it, the Lord hath spoken it.

The Lord God will wipe a - way

tears from off all fac - es, the Lord God will wipe away tears from off all fac - es, the Lord God, the Lord God will wipe away .. tears, .. will

add. Oboe.

rall. e dim.

wipe a - way tears from off all fac - es. . .

rall. e dim.

rall. e dim.

Isaiah xxvi. 3.

W. HATELY.

Quietly.

Thou wilt keep him in per - fect peace, whose mind is stayed, is

stayed on Thee, . . Thou wilt keep him in per - fect peace, whose

mind, whose mind is stayed on Thee: be - cause he

be - cause he trusteth, he

trusteth in Thee, be - cause he trusteth in Thee, he trust -

trusteth in Thee, be - cause he trusteth, he trusteth in Thee,

- eth, he trusteth in Thee, he trusteth, he trusteth in Thee. be -

poco rall. e dim.   *a tempo.*
pp sempre.

- cause   he   trusteth, he   trusteth   in   Thee. . .   Thou   wilt

poco rall. e dim.   *pp sempre.*

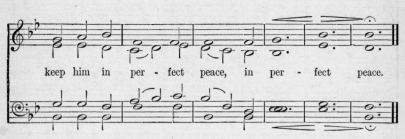

keep   him   in   per - fect   peace,   in   per - fect   peace.

74   Thou wilt keep him in perfect peace.

Isaiah xxvi. 3.   H. J. GAUNTLETT.
Andantino.

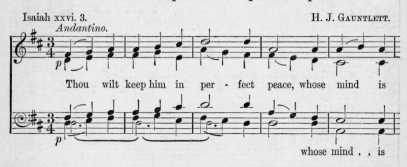

p

Thou   wilt keep him   in   per - fect   peace, whose   mind   is

whose mind . . is

p

stayed   on   Thee, . .   Thou   wilt keep him   in
          Thee,   on Thee,

cres.

stayed   on   Thee, . . .

cres.

Behold! a King shall reign.

Isaiah xxxii. 1, 2.

Andante maestoso. (♩ = 60.)

M. B. FOSTER.

f With Reeds.

Ped.

Sw.

Gt. *f*

- hold! be - hold! a King shall reign in righteousness, a

King shall reign in right - eous - ness, and princes shall

rule .. in .. judgment, *cres.* princes shall rule .. in

cres.

cres.

judg - ment.

ff

And a man shall be as an hid - ing-place from the wind,

a man shall be as an hid - ing - place .. from the wind, ..

and a covert   from the tem - pest,   and a covert

Full Swell closed.

O Zion, that bringest good tidings.*

Isaiah xl. 9.

J. STAINER,

Al - le - lu - ia, Al - le - lu - ia, Al - le - lu - ia, O

Zi - on, that bringest good tid - ings, get thee up, get thee up in - to the high

moun - tain. Al - le - lu - ia, Al - le - lu - ia, Al - le - lu - -
Al - le - lu - ia,

- ia. O Je - ru - salem, that bringest good tid - ings, lift up thy

lift up thy voice, be not a -
voice, thy voice with strength; lift up thy voice,
be not a - fraid,

* The first movement may be used as a separate Anthem.

* If G is found too high, D may be sung.

* Very slowly and smoothly. (♩. = 50.)

pp (Pastorale.)

SOPRANOS ONLY.

pp

O   that Birth for ev - er bless - ed, When the

Vir - gin, full   of grace,   By the   Ho - ly Ghost conceiv - ing, Bare the

cres.

f

Sa - viour of   our race,   And   the Babe, the world's Redeem - er, First re-

cres.

f

* It is suggested that stops of the Hautboy and Flute quality should be used for this movement.

(194)

- veal'd His sa - cred Face, Ev - er - more and ev - er-more.

TENORS.

Of the Fa-ther's Love be - got - ten Ere the

BASSES.

Of the Fa-ther's Love be - got - ten Ere the

worlds be - gan to be, He is Al - pha and O - me - ga, He the

worlds be - gan to be, He is Al - pha and O - me - ga, He the

Repeat first Chorus, and there end.

77 **He shall feed His flock.**

Isaiah xl. 11.   J. ALLAN.

They that wait upon the Lord.

Isaiah xl. 31 ; xxvi. 4.

G. J. ELVEY.

Con moto.

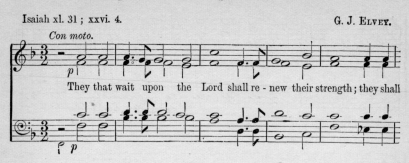

They that wait upon the Lord shall re - new their strength; they shall

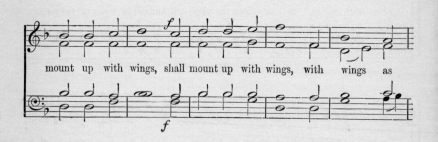

mount up with wings, shall mount up with wings, with wings as

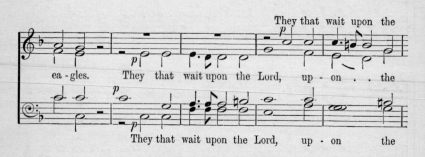

ea - gles. They that wait upon the Lord, up - on . . the

They that wait upon the Lord, up - on the

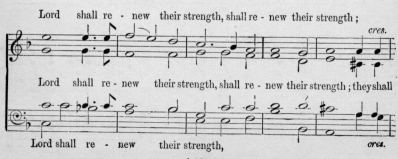

Lord shall re - new their strength, shall re - new their strength;

Lord shall re - new their strength, shall re - new their strength; they shall

Lord shall re - new their strength,

mount up with wings, shall mount up with wings, shall mount up with

with wings as . . ea - gles;

wings, with wings as ea - gles; they shall run, and not be wea - ry; they shall

walk, and not be faint; they shall run, and not be wea - ry; shall

walk, and not be faint, they shall walk, and not be faint. . .

A little faster.

Trust ye in the Lord, in the Lord for ev - er; for in the

Lord Je - ho - vah is ev - erlast - ing strength, trust ye in the

for in the Lord . . Je

Lord, in the Lord . . for ev - er; for in the Lord Je

for in the

- ho - vah is ev - er - last - ing strength,

Lord Je - ho - vah is ev - er-last - ing strength,

- ho - vah is ev - er - last - ing strength, trust

Lord Je - ho - vah is ev - er-last - ing strength,

trust ye in the Lord, in the Lord Je - ho - vah; for in the Lord Je -

trust ye in the Lord, in the Lord Je - ho - vah;

- ho - vah is ev - er-last-ing strength, ev - er last - ing strength.

79   O that thou hadst hearkened.

Isaiah xlviii. 18.

Slowly and tenderly.

Arranged from GOUNOD by J. B. THOMSON.

O that thou hadst hearkened, O that thou hadst hearkened, hadst heark - en - ed to My commandments ; then had thy peace been as a riv - er, and thy righteousness as the waves, .. as the waves, the waves of the sea, then had thy peace been as a riv - er, and thy righteousness as the waves, as the waves of the sea.

80 Who is among you that feareth the Lord.

Isaiah l. 10.

H. G. Trembath.

TENORS AND BASSES.

mp Who is among you that fear - eth the Lord, who is among you that fear - eth the Lord, that o - bey - eth the voice of His ser - vant, that walk - eth in dark - ness, and hath no light?

Moderato. (♩= 60.)

rit. e cres. poco.

81 How beautiful upon the mountains.

Isaiah lii. 7, 9.

R. A. SMITH.

Moderato.

How beauti-ful up-on the mountains,

How beautiful upon the

how beautiful upon the mountains are the feet of him that

mountains,

bringeth good tidings, that publisheth peace, that publisheth peace; that

bringeth good tidings, good tidings of good, that publisheth sal - vation; that

saith un - to Zi - on, Thy God reigneth, Thy God reign - eth!

Break forth in - to joy, sing to - gether, sing to - gether, ye waste plac - es of Je - ru - sa - lem: for the Lord hath comforted His peo - ple, He hath re - deem - ed Je - ru - sa - lem. Halle - lu - jah, Halle - lu - jah. Praise ye the Lord; Halle - lu - jah, Halle - lu - jah. Praise ye the Lord.

* This repeat is optional

Break forth into joy.

Isaiah lii. 9, 10.

R. S. Barnicott.

- ge - ther, ye waste plac -es of Je - ru - sa-lem, of Je - ru - sa - lem. . .

ALL VOICES IN UNISON.

The Lord hath made bare His ho - ly arm, . . the

Lord hath made bare His ho - ly arm . . in the

eyes of all the na - tions, in the eyes of all the na - -

and all the ends of the earth . . shall see the sal -

- tions ; and all . . the ends of the earth . . shall . . see the sal -

ye .. waste plac - es, ye .. waste plac - es, sing to - ge - ther,

sing to - ge - ther, ye waste plac - es of Je - ru - sa - lem, of Je -

- ru - sa - lem . . . . And all the ends of the earth . . .

legato.

shall . . see the sal - va-tion, sal - va - tion of God, shall

see the sal - va - tion, shall see the sal - va - tion of

God.

83 For a small moment have I forsaken thee.

Isaiah liv. 7, 8, 10.

J. STAINER.

Slowly. (♩ = 60.)

pp
For a small moment have I for-sak-en thee; but with great mercies will I ga - ther thee. In a lit-tle wrath I hid my face from thee for a moment; but with ev-er-last-ing kind-ness will I have mercy on thee, saith the Lord thy Re-deem - er.

QUARTET, OR SEMI-CHORUS.

Allegretto. (♩ = 100.)

p
For the mountains shall de - part, and the hills be re -

H

(213)

dim.

mov'd ; but My kind - ness shall not de - part from thee,

dim.

p

neither shall the covenant of My peace be re - mov - ed,

p

cres.

f

neither shall the covenant of My peace be re - mov - ed, saith the

cres.

f

ff

Lord, the Lord that hath mer - cy up - on . . thee, My kindness shall

ff

p

pp

rall.

not depart from thee, saith the Lord that hath mer - cy up - on . . thee.

pp

rall.

Repeat the Quartet, or Semi-Chorus, "For the mountains shall depart," as Chorus

(214)

Seek ye the Lord.

Isaiah lv. 6, 7.

J. F. Bridge.

Soprano Solo, or all the Sopranos.

Seek ye the Lord while . . He may be found, call ye up - on Him while He is near,

Chorus.
Seek ye the Lord while . . He may be found,

Seek ye the Lord while He may be found, . . call . . ye up -

found, call

found, . . call

call . . ye up - on Him while He is

- on Him while He is near, call ye up - on Him while He is

dim.

85   Seek ye the Lord.

Isaiah lv. 6, 7.

Moderato. (♩ = 60.)

QUARTET, OR SEMI-CHORUS.

F. R. RICKMAN.

Seek ye the Lord while He may be found, seek ye the Lord while He may be found, call ye up - on . . Him, call ye up - on . . Him, call ye up - on Him while He is near: Seek ye the Lord while He may be found, seek ye the Lord while He may be found, call ye up - on . . Him,

From *The Bristol Anthem Book*, by permission of Mr. W. Crofton Hemmons, Bristol.

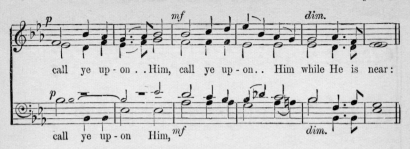

call ye up - on .. Him, call ye up - on .. Him while He is near:

call ye up - on Him,

TENORS AND BASSES.

Let the wick - ed for -

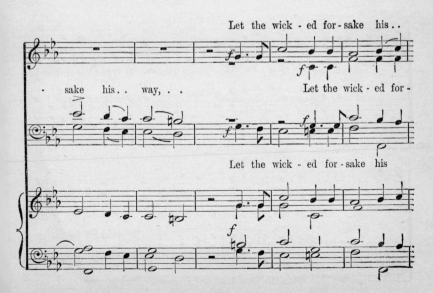

Let the wick - ed for - sake his ..

- sake his .. way, .. Let the wick - ed for -

Let the wick - ed for - sake his

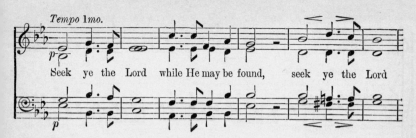

Seek ye the Lord while He may be found, seek ye the Lord

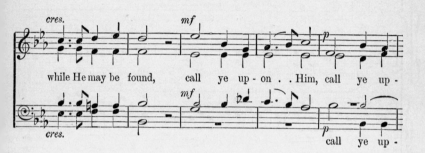

while He may be found, call ye up - on . . Him, call ye up -

call . . . . call ye up -

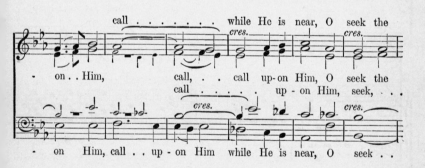

call . . . . while He is near, O seek the

- on . . Him, call, . . call up-on Him, O seek the

call . . . . . up - on Him, seek, . . .

- on Him, call . . up - on Him while He is near, O seek . .

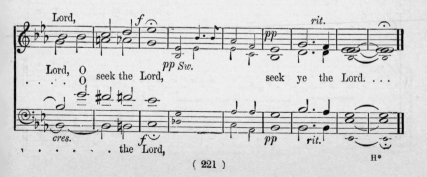

Lord,

Lord, O seek the Lord, seek ye the Lord. . . .

. . . . . . the Lord,

H*

Seek ye the Lord.

Isaiah lv. 6, 7.

J. V. ROBERTS.

He is near,   seek ye the Lord,

seek   the Lord,   seek ye the Lord while He may . . be

seek ye the Lord,   while He   is near :

found,   call ye up - on Him while He   is   near :

SEEK YE THE LORD.

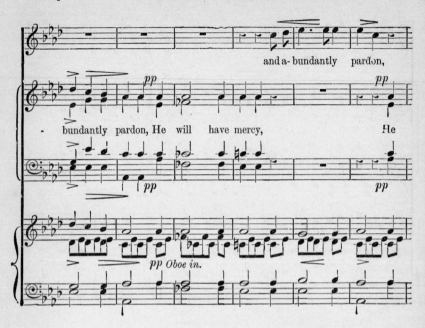

and a- bundantly pardon,

- bundantly pardon, He will have mercy,

He

pp   pp   pp   pp Oboe in.

and a- bund- ant-ly par-don.   A - men.

will   have   mer-cy and   par - don.   A - men.

rall.

Ped. 32 ft

87 Arise, shine, for thy light is come.

Isaiah lx. 1—3.

G. J. ELVEY.

A - rise, a - rise, shine, shine, for thy light is come, shine,

A - rise, a - rise, shine, for thy light is come,

shine, for thy light is come, is

shine, for thy light is come, and the glo - ry of the Lord is ris -

shine, for thy light is come, and the glo - ry of the Lord is

ris - en up - on thee, is ris - - - en up - on . . thee.

ris - en up - on thee, is ris - en, is ris - en up - on . . thee.

ris - en up - on thee,

For behold, darkness shall cov - er the earth, and gross

(229)

darkness,   and gross darkness,   gross dark - ness the

people,   gross dark - ness the peo - ple: but the

Lord shall a - rise,   the Lord shall a - rise,   the Lord shall a -

shine, for thy light is come, shine, for thy light is come, thy light is come.

shine, for thy light is come, shine, for thy light is come, thy light . . is come.

. . . for thy light is come, shine,

shine, for thy light is come, shine, for thy light is come, thy light is come.

88   Arise, shine, for thy light is come.

Isaiah lx. 1, 19.

E. J. HOPKINS

Bold and spirited. (= 116.)

A-rise, shine, for thy light is come, and the glory of the

Lord, the glo-ry of the Lord, the glo-ry of the Lord, is

ris-en up-on thee, a-rise, shine, for thy light is come, and the

glo-ry of the Lord, the glo-ry of the Lord is ris -.

In all their affliction.

Isaiah lxiii. 9.

W. J. Hutchins.

In all their af-flic-tion He was af-flict-ed, and the an-gel of His presence saved them: in His love and in His pi-ty He re-deem-ed them, He re-deem-ed them; and He bare them, and He

and car-ried them all the days of old, and He bare them, and

bare them, carried them all the days of old, bare them,

car-ried them, carried them, He car ried them all the days of old, all the days of old.

Thou, O Lord, art our Father.

Isaiah lxiii. 16 ; John iv. 23.

J. BARNBY.

Thou, O Lord, art our Fa - ther, Thou, Thou art our Fa - ther;

our Re - deem - er from ev - er - last - ing is . . Thy name.

Thou, . . Thou, O Lord, art our Fa - ther, . . Thou art . . our

Thou, O Lord,

Fa - ther; our Re - deem - er from ev - er - last - ing, our Re -

- deem - er from ev - er - last - ing is Thy name, . . is

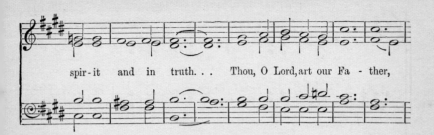

spir-it   and   in   truth. . .   Thou, O Lord, art our Fa - ther,

Thou . .   art   our   Fa - ther ;   our   Re - deemer from ev - er -

f our   Re - deem

-- last - ing   is   Thy   name,   our   Re - deem - er,

-- er   is   Thy   name,

our   Re - deem - er   from   ev - er - last - ing   is   Thy   name.

Lamentations iii. 22, 23 ; Psalms lxviii. 19 ; xxxvi. 10.

J. Booth.

It is of the Lord's mercies that we are not con - sum - ed, be -
cause His compassions fail not. They are new ev - ery morn - ing,
great is Thy faith - ful - ness. Blessed, blessed, bless - ed be the
Lord, . . who dai - ly load - eth us with His ben - e - fits,
e - ven the God, the God of our sal - va - tion, e - ven the God, the

God of our sal-va - tion.

O con-tinue Thy lov - ing-kindness, Thy lov - ing-kindness un-to them that know Thee; and Thy righteousness to the upright in heart, and Thy righteousness to the upright in heart. A - men.

The Lord is my portion.

Lamentations iii. 24—26.

E. J. HOPKINS.

Moderato. (♩ = 72.)

The Lord is my por - tion, saith my soul; .. therefore will I hope, will I hope in Him. The Lord .. is good unto them .. that wait for Him, to the soul .. that seeketh Him, that seek - eth Him, the Lord is good unto them .. that wait for Him, to the soul that seeketh Him, that seek - eth Him. It is good that a man should both

A little quicker.

hope and qui-et-ly wait, should qui-et-ly wait for the sal-

-vation of the Lord, a man should both hope .. and qui-et-ly

wait, .. and qui-et-ly wait for the sal-vation of the Lord, should

should

dim. *rall.* *Original time.*

qui-et-ly wait for the sal-va-tion of the Lord. The

dim. *rall.*

qui-et-ly wait . . . . for . . . the Lord.

cres.

Lord is my por-tion, saith my soul; therefore will I

cres.

hope, will I hope .. in Him, .. therefore will I hope, will I

hope .. in .. Him, will I hope in Him, will I hope in Him.

93

Daniel xii. **3.**

They that be wise.

J. M. Bell.

Firmly, and not too slow. ($\circ$ = 60).

They that be wise shall shine as the brightness, shine as the brightness of the

fir - ma - ment; they that be wise, they that be wise .. shall shine as the

brightness of the fir - ma - ment, shine as the brightness of the

fir - ma - ment; and they that turn ma - ny, turn ma - ny to

righteousness, and they that turn ma - ny, turn ma - ny to

Rather faster. ($\circ$ = 96.)

righteousness as the stars for ev - er and ev - er, the

stars for ev - er and ev - er, as the stars for .. ev - er and

ev - er, the stars for ev - er and ev - er, for

ev - er and ev - er, for ev - er and ev - er.

Come, and let us return.

Hosea vi. 1 ; Isaiah lv. 7 ; Psalm cxvi. 1—5.

W. Jackson.

Slowly and expressively.

Come, and let us re - turn.. un - to .. the Lord, and

He will have mer - cy, have mer - cy up - on us; and to our
and He will have

have mer - cy up - on us;

God, for He will a - bund - ant - ly par - don.

Sopranos. *A little faster.*

I love the Lord, be - cause He hath heard my voice, and my suppli -

A little faster.

ca - tions. Be - cause He hath in - clin - ed His ear un - to me, ..

therefore will I call . . up - on Him as long as I live, will

call . . up - on Him as long as I live.

ALL VOICES IN UNISON. *alla recit.*

mf The sorrows of death

com-pass'd me, the pains of hell gat hold up - on me: I found

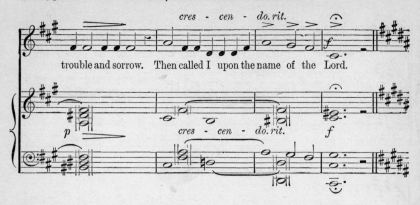

trouble and sorrow. Then called I upon the name of the Lord.

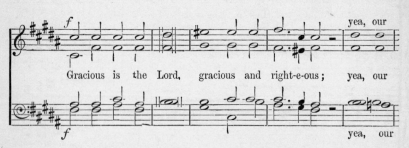

Gracious is the Lord, gracious and right-e-ous; yea, our

yea, our

God is mer - ci - ful.

God is mer - ci - ful.
God is mer - ci - ful. Who is like un-to the

God is mer - ci - ful.

Lord our God? Come, and let us re-turn un-to.. the

Joel ii. 13.

J. B. CALKIN.

Rend your heart, and not your garments, and turn un-to.. the

Lord your God: for He is gra - cious, gra - cious and mer - ci - ful,
for He is gra - cious and mer - ci - ful,

and re - pent - - eth
slow to an - ger, and of great kind - ness, and re - pent-eth

Him . . . of the e - vil,
Him . . of the e - vil, and re - pent - - eth Him, . .

cres.

and . . re - pent-eth Him of the e - vil.

Who is a God like unto Thee.

Micah vii. 18.

W. HATELY.

Moderato.

Who is a God like un-to Thee, who is a God like un-to

Thee, that par-doneth in-i-qui-ty, that par-doneth in-i-qui-ty, and

passeth by the transgression of the remnant of His her-it-age, and

passeth by the transgression of the remnant of His her-it-age?

Who is a God like un-to Thee? He re-taineth not His an-ger for

WHO IS A GOD LIKE UNTO THEE.

The Lord is good.

Nahum i. 7

First time QUARTET, *second time* CHORUS.

J. BELL.

The Lord is good, the Lord is good, a strong - hold, a strong - hold in the day .. of trou - ble, in the

day of trou - ble.

The Lord is good, the Lord is good, a strong - hold, the strong -hold,

Lord is good, a strong-hold, a strong-hold, a strong- hold in the the Lord is good,

day of trou - ble, the day .. of trou - ble.

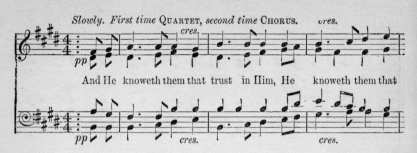

And He knoweth them that trust in Him, He knoweth them that

trust in Him, He knoweth them that trust in Him, He knoweth,

He

He

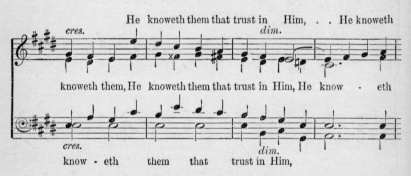

He knoweth them that trust in Him, . . He knoweth

knoweth them, He knoweth them that trust in Him, He know - eth

know - eth them that trust in Him,

them that trust, that trust in Him. Him.

them that trust, that trust in Him. Him. A - men.

Habakkuk ii. 20.

Slowly.

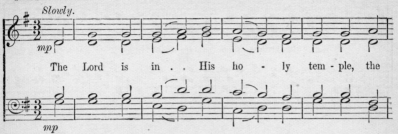

The Lord is in . . His ho - ly tem - ple, the

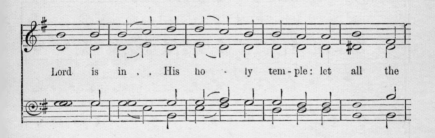

Lord is in . . His ho - ly tem - ple: let all the

earth keep si - lence be - fore Him, let all . . the earth keep

si - lence be - fore Him, keep si - lence be - fore Him.

Sing, O daughter of Zion.

Zephaniah iii. 14, 15.

H. E. BUTTON.

Allegro.

f Sing, sing, O daughter of Zi-on; shout, shout, O Is-ra-el;

sing, sing, O daughter of Zi-on; be glad and re-joice with all .. the

be glad and re-joice, be glad and re-joice with all . .the

mf be glad and re-joice, be glad and re-joice, O

heart, be glad and re-joice, be glad and re-joice with all . . the

be glad, re-joice, be glad, re-joice with all the

heart,

daughter, O daughter of Je-ru-salem, be glad, . . re-joice . .
heart,

heart,

with all the heart, O daughter .. of Je - ru - sa - lem.

O daughter of Je - ru - sa - lem.

* QUARTET. *Andante moderato.*

The Lord is in .. the midst of thee : .. thou shalt not see
ev - il an - y more, the Lord is in .. the midst of thee :

thou shalt not see ev - il, thou shalt not see ev - il, *dim.*

thou shalt not see ev - il, thou shalt not see ev - il, thou shalt not see

* If possible, this movement should be sung unaccompanied.

(257)

Rejoice greatly.

Zechariah ix. 9 ; Matthew xxi. 9 ;
Malachi iii. 2 ; Psalm xx. 9.

H. H. WOODWARD.

Re - joice greatly, O .. daughter of Zi - on : be -

- hold, thy King cometh un - to thee, .. re - joice, re -

- joice, be - hold, thy King cometh un - to thee : He is

just,　and　having sal - va - tion, He is just,　and　having sal -

- va - tion. Ho - san - na to the Son　of　Da - vid:

Blessed is He that cometh　in the name . . of the Lord. . . .

Quartet. Slow. (♩ = 69.)

But who may a - bide the day of His com - ing? and

But who may a - bide His com - ing?

Chorus. Largo. (♩ = 60.)

who shall stand when He . . ap - pear - eth? Save, Lord, and

cres. dim.

hear us, O King of Heaven, when we call up - on . . Thee.

cres. dim.

101 From the rising of the sun.

Malachi i. 11.   F. A. G. OUSELEY.

Moderato.

From the ris-ing of the sun un - to the going down of the

My name shall be great, shall be great a - mong . . the Gen -

same   My name shall be great
My name shall be great, shall be great

a - mong the Gen -

My name shall be great

a - mong the Gen -

From the ris - ing of the sun un - to the going down of the

My name shall be great, shall be great a - mong ..

same My name shall be great, shall be great a -

My name shall be great

My name shall be great a -

... the Gen - tiles;

-mong the Gen - tiles; and in ev' - ry place, and in

-mong the Gen - tiles;

un -

ev' - ry place in -cense shall be of -fer'd up un - to ..

un -

un -

- to .. My name, thus .. saith the Lord.

.. My name, thus .. saith the Lord.

-to ... My .. name, thus saith ... the Lord.

-to ... My name, thus saith the Lord.

Consider the lilies.

Matthew vi. 28, 29.

H. G. TREMBATH.

Con - sider the lil - ies of the field, how they grow; they toil not, they

toil not, neither do . . they spin, con - sider the lil - ies, con - sider the

neither do they spin, . .

lil - ies of the field, how they grow; they toil not, they toil not, neither

and yet I say unto you,
do . . they spin: and yet . . I say un-to you, That even
and yet . . I say . . un-to you,

and yet . . I . . say un-to you,

Sol - o-mon in all his glo - ry, ev - en Sol - o-mon in all his

103. I came not to call the righteous.

Matthew ix. 13 ; Luke xv. 10 ; 1 Timothy i. 15.

C. VINCENT.

I CAME NOT TO CALL THE RIGHTEOUS.

came not to call the right - eous, but sin - - ners to re -

- pent - ance.

QUARTET, OR SEMI-CHORUS.

There is joy in the presence of the an - gels of God ov - er

CHORUS.

one sin - ner that re - pent - eth, There is joy in the presence of the

ALL THE VOICES IN UNISON.

Christ Je - sus, Christ Je - sus came in - to the world to save . . sin - ners, Christ Je - - sus came in - to the world to save . . sin - - - - - ners.

Faith - ful, faith - - ful, faith - ful is the
say - - ing, and worth - y, and worth - y of
all ac - cep - ta - tion. A - men, A - men.

104   Come unto Me.

Matthew xi. 28, 29.   Arranged from GOUNOD by J. B. THOMSON.

Slowly.

Come un-to Me, come un-to Me, all ye that la-bour and

are heavy lad - en, and I will give, will give you rest, and

I will give, will give you rest. . . Take My yoke up -

- on you, and learn of Me; for I am meek and low - ly in

heart: and ye shall find rest un - to your souls, ye shall find

dim.

O come, ..

rest, ye shall find rest un - to your .. souls.

O

.. come un - to Me, O come, .. come un - to

come, come un - to Me, . O come, come un - to

Me,

Me, and I will give you rest, and I will give you rest.

ritard.

105 **Come unto Me.**

Matthew xi. 28—30.

J. Booth.

Largo. *Andante con moto.*

Come un - to Me, Come un - to Me, all ye that la - bour

and are heavy lad - en, are heavy lad - en, and I will give you

Hosanna to the Son of David.

Matthew xxi. 9.

Allegro maestoso.

J. B. CALKIN.

Ho - san - na, Ho - san - na, Ho - san - na to the Son of Da - vid, to the Son of Da - vid: Blessed is He that com - eth, that cometh in the name of the Lord, in the name of the Lord; . . Ho - san - na, Ho - san - na, Ho - san - na in the high - - est. A - men. . .

107 Suffer the little children.

Mark x. 14.

H. GADSBY.

Not too slowly.

108   Suffer the little children.

Mark x. 14, 15.

E. PROUT.

109 My soul doth magnify the Lord.

(MAGNIFICAT.)

Luke i. 46—55.

E. BUNNETT.

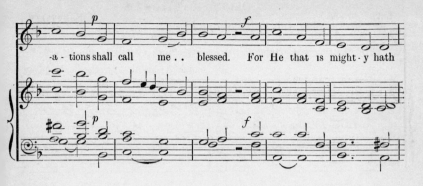

-a - tions shall call me .. blessed. For He that is might - y hath

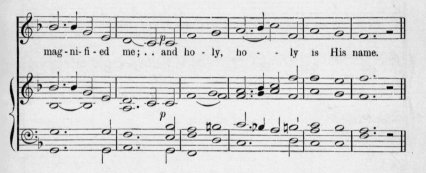

mag - ni - fi - ed me; .. and ho - ly, ho - - ly is His name.

The harmonized portions may be sung either with or without accompaniment.

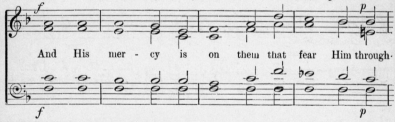

And His mer - cy is on them that fear Him through-

-out ... all gen - er - a - tions.

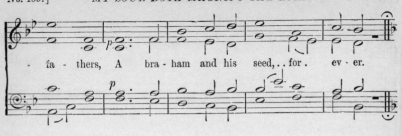

fa - thers, A bra - ham and his seed, . . for . ev - er.

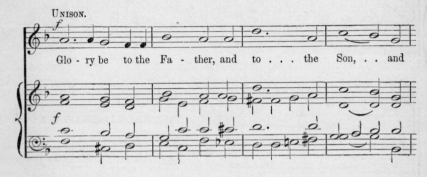

UNISON.

Glo - ry be to the Fa - ther, and to . . . the Son, . . and

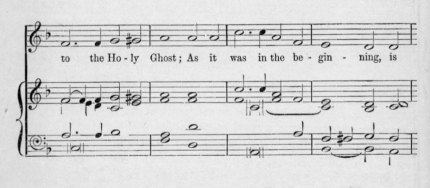

to the Ho - ly Ghost; As it was in the be - gin - ning, is

now and ev - er shall be: world with - out end. A - men.

My soul doth magnify the Lord.

Luke i. 46—55.   (MAGNIFICAT.)

J. STAINER.

Allegro.

Allegro. (♩ = 100.)

My soul doth mag - ni - fy the Lord, and my spir - it hath re -

- joic - ed in God my Sa - viour. For He hath re -

- gard - ed the low - li - ness .. of His hand - maid - en.

mf For .. be - hold, from hence - forth all gen - er - ations shall call me

bless - ed. For He that is might - y hath mag - ni - fi - ed   me; and

ho - ly .. is .. His   name. And His mer - cy is   on

them that fear   Him, throughout all gen - er - a - tions. He hath shewed

strength, shewed strength with His arn. · He hath scatter - ed the proud

in the im - ag - in - a - tion .. of their hearts.

He hath put down .. the might · y from their seat, and

hath ex - alt - ed the humble and meek. He hath fill - ed the

hun - gry, the hungry with good things; and the rich he hath sent

emp - ty a - way. He re - mem - b'ring His mer - cy hath

holpen His servant Is - ra-el; as He prom - ised to our fore -

- fa - thers, A - bra - ham and his seed, for ev - er.

Glo - ry be to the Fa - ther, and to the Son, and to the Ho ly Ghost; As it was in the be - gin - ning, is now, and ev - er shall be : world with - out end. A - men.

My soul doth magnify the Lord.

(MAGNIFICAT.)

Luke i. 46—55.

A. S. Marks.

For be-hold, from hence-forth all gen-er-a-tions shall call . . me bless-ed. For He that is might-y hath mag-ni-fied me; and ho-ly is His name.

VOICES IN UNISON.

And His mer - cy is on them, . . on them that . . fear Him, throughout all gen - er - a - tions. He hath shewed strength . . . . with His arm; He hath scat - ter-ed the proud in the im - ag - in - a - tion

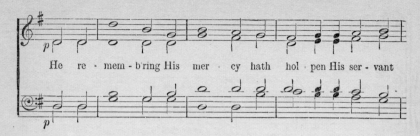

He re- mem- b'ring His mer - cy hath hol pen His ser - vant

Is - ra - el ;   as   He   prom - is - ed   to   our   fore --

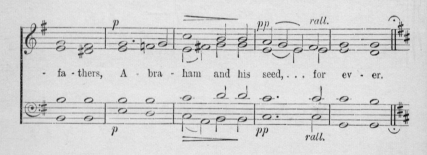

- fa - thers,   A - bra - ham and his   seed, . . . for   ev - er.

VOICES IN UNISON.

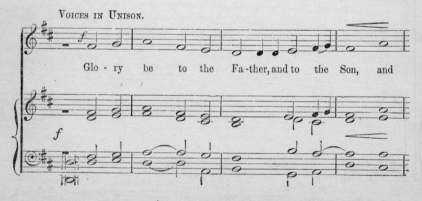

Glo - ry   be   to the Fa - ther, and to   the   Son,   and

to the Ho - ly Ghost; As it was in the be - gin - ning, is

now, and ev - er shall be: world with - out end. A - men.

112 Blessed be the Lord God of Israel.

Luke i. 68—79. (BENEDICTUS.)

J. Goss.

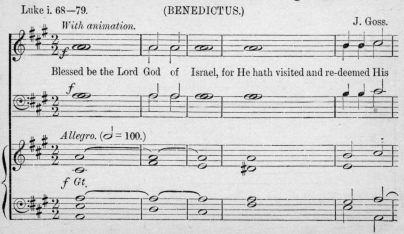

Blessed be the Lord God of Israel, for He hath visited and re-deemed His

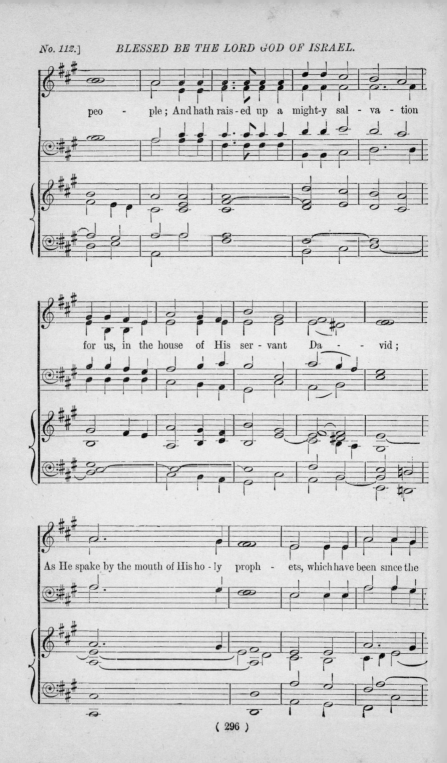

peo - ple ; And hath rais-ed up a might-y sal - va - tion

for us, in the house of His ser - vant Da - vid ;

As He spake by the mouth of His ho - ly proph - ets, which have been since the world be - gan: That we should be sav - ed from our

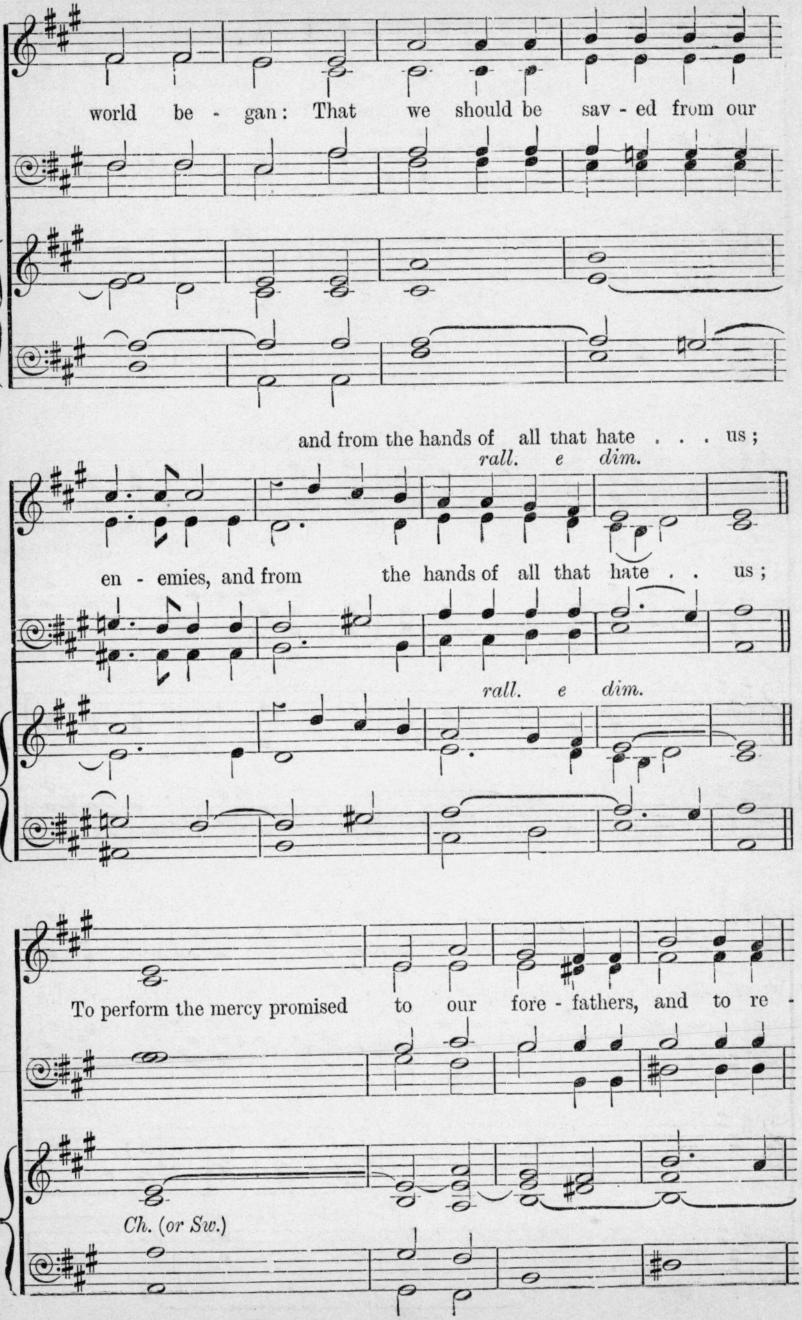

and from the hands of all that hate . . . us ;

rall. e dim.

en - emies, and from the hands of all that hate . . us ;

rall. e dim.

To perform the mercy promised to our fore - fathers, and to re -

Ch. (or Sw.)

- member His ho - ly covenant; To perform the oath which He

sware to our fore - fa - ther A - braham, that He . . . would *that He would*

that He would

give us, That we be-ing de - liv-er-ed out of the hand of our

enemies might serve Him without fear, In ho - li - ness and

dim.

right-eous - ness be - fore Him, all the days of our life.

And thou, child, .. shalt be call-ed the prophet of the Highest :

f

Gt.

for thou shalt go before the face of the Lord . . . to pre-

pare His ways; To give knowledge of sal - va - tion un - to His

Ch. (or Sw.)

peo - ple, for the re - mis - sion of their sins, Through the ten - der

dim.

mer-cy of our God; where-by the day-spring from on high hath

vis - it - ed us, To give light to them that sit in dark - ness,

and in the shad - ow . . of death, and to guide our

and in the shad - ow of . death,

and in the shad - ow . . of death,

feet . . . . in - to the way . . . of peace.

to guide our feet in - to the way . . of peace.

to guide our feet in - to the way . . . of peace.

With spirit.

Glo - ry be to the Fa - ther, and

With spirit. ($\textit{d} = 100$.)

to the Son, . . . and to the

Ho - - ly Ghost; As it was in the be -

- gin - ning, . . is now, and ev - er shall be: world

with - out end. . . . . . A - - men.

113   Blessed be the Lord God of Israel.

Luke i. 68—79.   (BENEDICTUS.)

Allegro moderato.   A. W. MARCHANT.

prophets, which have been   since the world   be - gan: . . That

we   should be   sav - ed from our   en - e - mies, and from the

hands of all that hate . .   us;   To per - form the mer - cy

... That we be-ing de-liv-er-ed out of the hand of our

en-emies might serve Him with-out .. fear, In ho-liness and

righteousness be-fore .. Him, all the days .. of our

life. . . And thou, child, shalt be call - ed the prophet of the

High - est: for thou shalt go be-fore the face . . of the

Lord to pre - pare His ways; . . To give knowledge of sal -

-va - tion .. un - to His peo - ple, . . for the re - mis - sion

of their sins, Through the ten - der mer - cy of our God; . . where-

- by the day - spring from . . on high, . . where - by the

day - spring . . from on high . . . . hath vis - it -

- ed . . . . . us,   To give

light . . . . to them that sit in dark - ness,

and in the shad - ow of death, . . .

and to guide our feet in - to the way . . of peace.

and to guide our feet in - to the way of peace.

a tempo. Without Organ.

Organ.

Without Ped.

Allegro moderato.

Glo - ry be to the Fa - ther, and . . to the

Allegro moderato.

Ped.

Son, and to the Ho - ly   Ghost; As it   was   in the be -

- gin - ning, is now, and ev - er   shall be: world with - out . .

end. A - - men, A - - men,   A - men.

114 Behold, I bring you good tidings.

Luke ii. 10, 11.

J. Goss.

115 Let us now go even unto Bethlehem.

Luke ii. 15, 10, 11.

J. L. HATTON.

Let us now go ev-en un-to Beth-lehem, and see this thing which is come to pass, which the Lord hath made known, which the which the Lord hath made known, which the Lord hath made known, hath made known, known, which the Lord hath made known, hath made known,

made known un - to us.

Trumpet.

Allegro moderato.

For the an - gel said un - to us,

Allegro moderato.

of   great   joy.

Trumpet.

Without Pedal.

ff   For un-to you   is born this day   in the ci-ty of Da-vid

ff

(Trump.)

ff

Ped.

pp

a   Sav - iour

pp

Without Organ.

Without Pedal.   *Ped.*

Lord, now lettest Thou Thy servant.

(NUNC DIMITTIS.)

Luke ii. 29—32.

E. Bunnett.

Slowly. ALL THE VOICES IN UNISON.

Lord, now lettest Thou Thy ser-vant de-part.. in peace, in peace, ac-cord-ing to Thy word:.. For mine eyes have seen, have seen Thy sal-va-tion, Which Thou hast pre-par-ed be-fore the face of all peo-ple; To

be a light to light - en the Gen - tiles, and to be the

glo - ry of Thy peo-ple Is - ra - el. Glo - ry be to the Fa - ther, and

to the Son, . . and to the Ho-ly Ghost; As it was in the be

- gin - ning, is now, and ev -er shall be: world without end. A - men.

117 Lord, now lettest Thou Thy servant.

(NUNC DIMITTIS.)

Luke ii. 29—32.   J. STAINER.

Moderato.

Lord, now let - test Thou Thy ser - vant de - part . . in peace, ac - cord - ing to Thy . . word: For mine eyes have seen Thy sal - va - tion, Which Thou hast pre - pared before the

Moderato. (♩ = 100.)

(326)

be to the Fa - ther, and to . . the Son, and to the

Ho - ly Ghost; As it was in the be - gin - ning, is now, and ev - er

shall be : world without end. A - men, A - men, A - men.

118   Lord, now lettest Thou Thy servant.

Luke ii. 29—32.   (NUNC DIMITTIS.)   A. S. MARKS.

Lord, now lettest Thou Thy servant de - part in peace, ac - cord - ing to Thy word: .. For mine eyes have seen, have seen Thy sal - va - tion, Which Thou hast pre - par - ed be - fore the face of all peo - ple; To be a light to light - en the Gen - - tiles, and to be the

Let your loins be girded.

Luke xii. 35, 36.

G. F. Cobb.

Larghetto. (♩ = 96.)

Let your loins be gird - ed, be gird - ed a - bout, and your lamps, your lamps . . . burn - ing, let your loins be gird - ed, be gird - ed a - bout, and your lamps burn - ing, your lamps

burning, let your loins be gird - ed, and your lamps . .

burning; and be ye . . your - selves, . . be ye . . your -

- selves like un - to men that look for their lord, that

look for their lord, and be ye . . your - selves like

men, like men that look, that look for their lord.

120

I will arise.

Luke xv. 18, 19.

R. Cecil.

I will a - rise, I will a - rise and go to my Fa - ther, and will say un - to Him, Fa - ther, Fa - ther, I have sinned, have sinned, I have sinned against heaven, and be-fore Thee, and am no more wor-thy to be call - ed Thy son. I will a - rise, I will a - rise and go to my Fa - ther, my Fa - ther.

John i. 29.
Slowly.

A. E. GRELL.

Be-hold the Lamb of God, the Lamb of God, be-hold the Lamb of God, be-hold the Lamb of God, which tak-eth a-way the sin of the world, which tak-eth a-way.. the sin of the world. Be-hold the Lamb of God be-hold the Lamb, the Lamb of God, which tak-eth a-way the sin of the world, which tak-eth a-way the

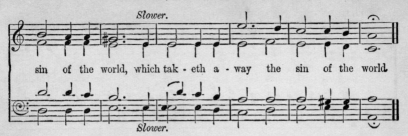

sin of the world, which tak - eth a - way the sin of the world.

122   God so loved the world.

John iii. 16, 17.

J. STAINER.

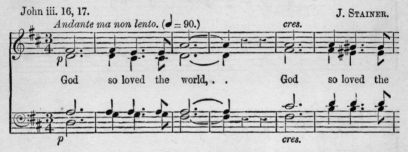

God   so loved the world, . .   God   so loved the

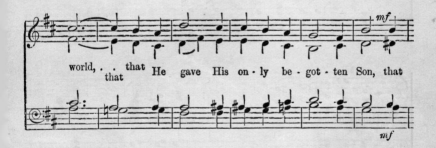

world, . . that He gave His on - ly be - got - ten Son, that

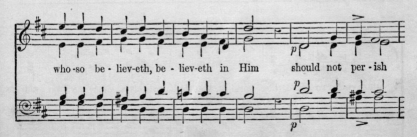

who -so be - liev-eth, be - liev-eth in Him   should not per - ish

This Anthem should, if possible, be sung without Accompaniment.

GOD SO LOVED THE WORLD.

should not per-ish, but have ev-er-last-ing life. For God

sent not His Son in-to the world to con-demn the world, God sent not His

Son in-to the world to con-demn the world; but that the world through

Him might be sav-ed. God so loved the world, . .

God so loved the world, . . that He gave His on-ly be-got-ten
that

Son, that who-so be-liev-eth, be-liev-eth in Him should not per-ish, should not per-ish, but have ev-er-last-ing life, ev-er-last-ing life, ev-er-last-ing, ev-er-last-ing life. God so loved the world, . . God so loved the world, . . God so loved the world.

God is a Spirit.

John iv. 23, 24.

H. SMART.

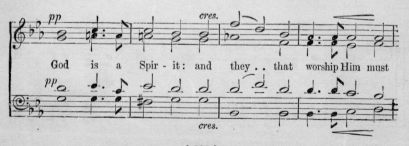

124   **Jesus said unto the people.**

John vi. 33—35.

J. STAINER.

Je - sus said un - to the peo - ple, The bread of God is He which com - eth down from heaven, and

(340)

giv - eth life, and giv - eth life, life un -

- to the world. Then said they un - to

Him, Lord, . . ev - ermore give us . . . this bread.

Me . . shall nev - er hun - ger; and he that be -

· hev - eth on Me shall nev - er, nev - er er
nev - er

thirst, shall nev - er thirst, shall nev - er

thirst. A - men, A - men. . . .

126   I will not leave you comfortless.

John xiv. 18—21.

B. STEANE.

Andante grazioso. (♩ = 50.)

I will not leave you com-fort-less, I will not leave you com-fort-less: I will .. come to you. Yet a lit-tle while, and the world seeth Me no more, seeth Me no more; but ye .. see Me: be-cause I live, .. ye shall live .. al-so. At that day ye shall know that I am in My Fa-ther, and

127 And it shall come to pass in the last days.

Acts ii. 17, 18, 21.

M. B. FOSTER

prophesy, . . your sons and your daugh - ters shall pro - phe - sy, . . and your young men shall see . . vi - sions, and your old men shall dream dreams, shall see visions, shall dream

Lord . . shall be sav-ed, shall be sav-ed, that who-so-ever, who-so-ev-er shall call on the name of the Lord, on the name of the Lord

Full Swell.

Gt. Diapasons.

Romans vi. 9.

Quartet, or Semi-Chorus.

G. J. Elvey.

Andante.

Christ be-ing rais-ed from the dead, Christ

Christ be-ing rais-ed from the dead,

Christ be-ing rais-ed from the dead,

Christ be-ing rais-ed from the dead, Christ be-ing

Christ be-ing rais-ed from the dead,

Christ be-ing rais - ed from .. the dead,

Christ be-ing rais - ed from the dead,

rais-ed, rais - ed from .. the dead,

di - eth no .. more, di - eth no ..

di-eth no more, di -

di-eth no more, di - eth no .. more,

di - eth no .. more, di -

more, di - eth no .. more, di - eth no .. more, di -

-eth no .. more,

di - eth no .. more, no more, ..

o - ver Him, no more do - min - - ion o . . .

· ver Him.

129 𝕮𝖍𝖗𝖎𝖘𝖙 𝖇𝖊𝖎𝖓𝖌 𝖗𝖆𝖎𝖘𝖊𝖉 𝖋𝖗𝖔𝖒 𝖙𝖍𝖊 𝖉𝖊𝖆𝖉.

Romans vi. 9—11.

Andante.

W. H. GILL.

mf

Christ being raised from the dead, di - eth no more, Christ being raised

mf

Ped.

di - eth no more,

from the dead, di - eth no more: death hath no more do-min-ion o - ver Him,

di - eth no more: *Ped. 8ve lower.*

death hath no more do - min - ion o - ver Him. For in that He

died, He died un - to sin once: but in . . that He

liv - eth, He liv - eth un - to God. Like-wise reck - on ye al - so your .

- selves to be dead . . in - deed un - to sin, but a - live un - to

God through Je - sus Christ our Lord. A - men, A - men.

130 How lovely are the messengers.

Romans x. 15, 18.

MENDELSSOHN.

Andante con moto. (♪ = 132.)

How love - ly are the mes - sen-gers that preach us the gospel of peace,

How love - ly are the mes - sen-gers that preach us the gospel of peace,

the gos - pel of peace, the messengers that preach . . us the

How lovely are the messengers that preach us the gospel of

gospel of peace, How love - - ly

peace, How love - ly are the mes - sen-gers that preach us the gospel of

cres.

HOW LOVELY ARE THE MESSENGERS.

gone forth the sound of their words, .. to all ... the

words, .. is gone forth the sound of their words, to all the

na - tions is gone forth the sound of their words, throughout all the

lands their glad tid - - ings... How love-ly are the messengers that

131

The night is far spent.

Romans xiii. 12.

T. HEWLETT.

Andante.

The night is far spent, .. the day is at hand: let us

there - fore, .. there - fore, let us there - fore cast a - way the works of dark -

- ness, the night is far spent, .. the day is at

hand: let us therefore cast off the works of dark - ness, cast off the

Without organ. *With organ.*

cast off the works of dark - ness, and let us put on,

works of dark - ness, .. and let us put

rall.

ness, ..

132 Christ our passover is sacrificed for us

1 Corinthians v. 7, 8.

J. Goss.

Moderato. ($\stackrel{.}{\bullet} = 66$.)

Christ.. our pass - o - ver is sac - ri - fic - ed for us:

therefore let us keep the feast, therefore let us keep the feast,

there - fore let us keep the feast,

SOPRANO SOLO. *Slower.*

not with the old leav - en, nor with the leav - en of

mal - ice and wickedness ; but with th'un-leav-ened bread of sin-

133 Christ is risen from the dead.

1 Corinthians xv. 20—22.

T. Smith.

Moderato.

Christ is ris - en from the dead, Christ is ris - en from the dead, and be -

-come the first-fruits of them . . that slept, and become the first-fruits of

them that slept. Christ is ris - en from the dead, Christ is ris - en

from the dead, and become the first-fruits of them that slept.

For since by man came death, for since by man came death, by man came

also the res - ur - rec-tion of the dead. For as in Adam all die,

for as in Adam all die, even so in Christ shall all be made a -

- live, ev - en so in Christ shall all be made a - live, ev - en

so in Christ shall all be made a - live, shall all, shall all be

made a - live. Al - le - lu - ia, Al - le - lu - ia. A - men.

Ephesians iv. 30—32.

J. STAINER.

QUARTET, OR SEMI-CHORUS.

Andante. (𝅗𝅥 = 80.)

He humbled Himself.

Philippians ii. 7, 8.

PALESTRINA.

Very slowly and sustained.

He hum-bled Him - self, . . and made Him-self of no . . rep-u-ta - - tion, and be-came o - -be-dient un - to death, ev - - en the death ev - en the death the death . . the . . . . death of . . the . . cross, He be - came o - be - dient un - to death, . . . the death . . of the cross.

Colossians iii. 2, 3.

J. E. WEST.

Andante. (♩ = 88.)

Set your af-fec-tion on things a-bove, on things a-bove, not on things on the earth, set . . your af-fec-tion on things a-bove, on things a-bove, not on things on the earth. For ye are dead, for ye are dead, and your life is hid with Christ in God, your life is hid with Christ in God.

137   I know whom I have believed.

2 Timothy i. 12.

Andante maestoso. ($\bullet = 72$.)

G. A. Macfarren.

I know whom I have be - liev - ed, I know whom I have be - liev - ed, and am per - suad - ed that He is a - ble to keep . . . that . . which I have com - mit - ted un - to Him a - gainst . . that . . day, a - gainst . . that . . day. A - men, A - men.

James i. 12.

J. STAINER.

Allegro moderato.

Bless - ed is the man that en - dur - eth temp - ta - tion: for when he is tried, for when he is tried, he shall re - ceive the crown of life, which the Lord hath prom - is - ed to them that love . . . Him. . . Bless - ed is the man that en - dur - eth temp - ta - tion: for when he is tried, for

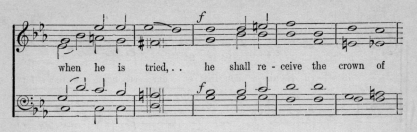

when he is tried, . . he shall re - ceive the crown of

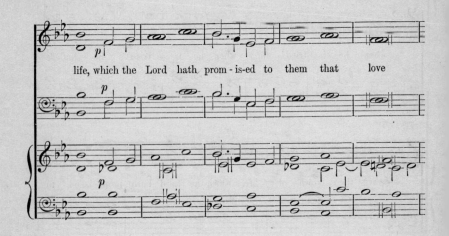

life, which the Lord hath prom - is-ed to them that love

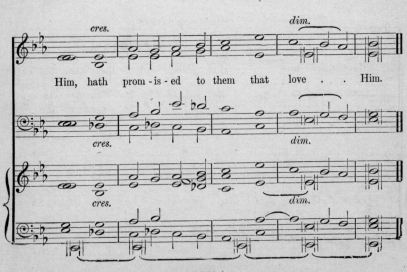

Him, hath prom - is - ed to them that love . . Him.

Beloved, let us love one another.

1 John iv. 7, 16.

G. F. COBB.

Be - lov-ed, let us love one an - other: for love .. is .. of God; .. and ev' - ry one that lov - eth is born of God, .. and know - eth

Be -

he .. that dwelleth, that dwelleth in love   dwelleth in God, and

CHORUS.
mf

And he that dwelleth, that dwelleth in love . .

CHORUS.

God in him... *mf*

dwell-eth in God, .. and God in him, . . dwelleth in God, and

f   *dim.*

f

dim.

dim.

God in him, .. dwell - eth in God, .. and God in him.

140 𝕭eloved, if 𝕲od so loved us.

1 John iv. 11, 21.

J. BARNBY.

Be - lov - ed, if God so loved us, . . we ought al - so to

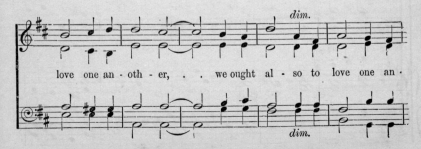

love one an - oth - er, . . we ought al - so to love one an -

(387)

- oth - er, . . Be - lov - ed, if God so loved us, . . Be -

we ought al - so to

lov - ed, if God so loved us, . . . we ought al - so,

we ought al - so to

love, . . . al - so to love, . . . al - so to love one an -

al - so to love, . . al - so to love, to love one an -

love, . . al - so to love, . . . al - so to love one an -

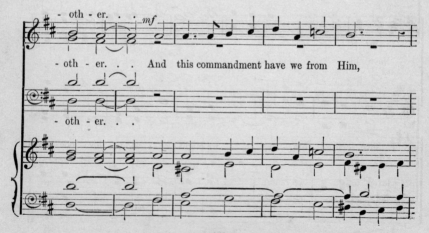

- oth - er. . . And this commandment have we from Him,

- oth - er. . .

Now unto Him.

Jude 24, 25.   L. Mason.

Moderato.

Now unto Him that is a-ble to keep you from fall-ing, and to pre-

-sent you faultless before the presence of His glo-ry with exceeding joy,

to the only wise God, our Sa-viour, be glo-ry and ma-jes-ty, do-

-min-ion and power, be glo-ry and ma-jes-ty, do-min-ion and

power, both now and ev-er. A - - - - men. . . .

Thou art worthy, O Lord.

Revelation iv. 11.

Boldly and with spirit.

E. PROUT.

Thou art worthy, O Lord, art worthy, O Lord, Thou art worthy, O Lord, to receive glo-ry and honour and power, glo-ry and hon-our and power, .. Thou art worthy, O Lord, to receive glo-ry and hon-our and power, to receive glo-ry, to receive power, to receive glo-ry and honour and power, glo-ry and hon-our and

mf to receive glo-ry, to receive honour,

THOU ART WORTHY, O LORD.

Worthy is the Lamb.

Revelation v. 12.

H. Smart.

Con moto moderato. (♩ = 54.)

Wor - thy is the Lamb, wor - thy is the Lamb that was
slain, . . was slain, slain, that was slain, to receive pow - er, and rich - es, and
slain, . . was slain, wis - dom, and strength, and hon - our, and glo - ry, and bless - ing.

wor - thy is the Lamb . . that was
Wor - thy is the Lamb, wor - thy is the Lamb that was
Lamb that was slain, that was
wor - thy is the Lamb that was slain, . . was
slain, slain, to receive pow - er, and rich - es, and wis - dom, and strength, and
slain.

WORTHY IS THE LAMB.

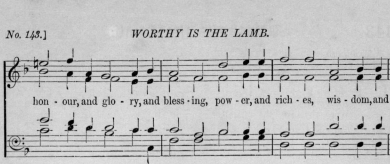

hon - our, and glo - ry, and bless - ing, pow - er, and rich - es, wis - dom, and

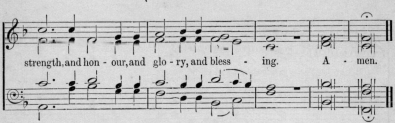

strength, and hon - our, and glo - ry, and bless - ing. A - men.

144   What are these.

Revelation vii. 13—17.

J. STAINER

Quickly. (♩ = 108.)

Hal - le - lu - jah, Halle - lu - jah, Halle - lu - jah. What are these, what are

these that are arrayed in white robes, and whence came they? whence came they?

Silent.

A little slower, and with expression. (♩ = 80.)

These are they which came out of great trib-u - la - tion, and have wash-ed their

robes, and made them white in the blood of the Lamb, the blood of the

Lamb, These are they which came out of great trib-u - la-tion, and have

wash - ed their robes, and made them white in the blood of the

Lamb, and have made them white in the blood of the Lamb.

Hal-le - lu - jah, Hal-le - lu - jah, Hal-le - lu - jah. There-fore are

(395)

WHAT ARE THESE.

they, are they be-fore the throne of God, and serve Him day and

A little slower.

night, day and night in His tem-ple. They shall hun-ger no

more, neither thirst an-y more; nei-ther shall the sun light on them,

They shall hunger no more, neither thirst an-y

nor an-y heat. They shall hunger, shall hunger no more, no

They shall hun - - ger . . . no . . .

more.

more. For the Lamb which is in . . the midst of the throne shall feed . .

more. For the Lamb which is in the midst of the throne shall feed, shall

Revelation xiv. 13.   J. Goss.

Moderato.

mf

I heard a voice from heaven say - ing un - to me, Write,

From henceforth bless - ed are the dead which die . . in the

Lord, bless - ed are the dead which die in the Lord:

Ev - en so, saith the Spir-it, ev - en so, saith the Spirit, for they

they rest, they rest from their la - -

rest from their labours, they rest, they rest from their la -

they rest . . . from their la - -

-bours, *f a tempo.*

-bours. I heard a voice from heaven say - ing un - to me, Write,

From henceforth blessed are the dead which die . . in the Lord, bless -

- - ed are the dead which die in the Lord, bless - ed are the

dead which die in the Lord. Ev - en so, saith the Spir-it,

ev - en so, saith the Spirit, for they rest from their labours, they rest, they

(399)

146   J heard a voice from heaven.

Revelation xiv. 13.   J. H. TENNEY.

Moderato.

dead which die in the Lord from hence - forth: Yea, saith the

Spirit, yea, saith the Spirit, that they . . may rest, that

they . . may rest, that they may rest from their la -

- bours, that they may rest, may rest from their la - bours;

and . . their works do fol - low them. A - - men.

Great and marvellous.

Revelation xv. 3, 4.

H. SMART.

Moderato. ($\bullet$ = 80.)

Great and marvellous are Thy works, Lord God Al-might - y;

Lord . .

Lord God Al - mighty;

just and true are Thy ways, Thou King, Thou King of saints.

Great and

Great and marvellous are Thy works, Lord God Al-might - y;

mar - - vellous are thy works, Lord God Al-might - y;

just and true are Thy ways, Thou King of saints, Thou King of saints.

just and true are Thy ways, . . Thou King, Thou King of saints

Who shall not fear, shall not fear,

Who shall not fear, shall not fear Thee, O Lord, and

and

glo - ri - fy Thy name, . . and glo - ri - fy Thy name? for Thou on - ly art

glo - ri - fy Thy name, and glo - ri - fy Thy name? for . .

Thou on - ly art ho - - ly, ho - ly. . .

ho - ly, Thou on - ly art ho - - ly, art ho - ly. . .

Thou on - ly art ho - ly, art ho - - ly, ho - ly. . .

148 The Spirit and the Bride say, Come.

Revelation xxii. 17.

E. PROUT.

Rather slowly.

The Spir - it and the Bride say, Come, The Spir - it and the Bride say,

Come. . . And let him that heareth say, Come, let him that heareth say,

Come. And let him that is a - thirst come, and let

Come.

And let him that is a - thirst, let

We praise Thee, O God.

(TE DEUM LAUDAMUS.)

W. JACKSON.

Boldly.

We praise Thee, O God, we ac-know-ledge Thee to be the Lord. All the earth doth wor-ship Thee, the Fa-ther ev-er-last-ing. To Thee all an-gels cry a-loud, the heavens, and all the powers therein. To Thee cher-u-bin and ser-a-phin con-tin-ual-ly do cry, Ho-ly, ho-ly, ho-ly, Lord God of Sab-a-oth;

Slower.

Slower.

Vir - gin's womb. When Thou hadst overcome the sharpness of death, Thou didst

o - pen the kingdom of heaven to   all   be - liev - ers. Thou

sittest   at the right hand of God,   in the glo - ry   of   the   Fa - ther.

We   believe that Thou shalt come to   be   our judge. We therefore pray Thee,

help   Thy   servants, whom Thou hast redeem - ed .. with   Thy   precious

blood. Make them to be numbered with Thy saints, in glo-ry ev-er-last - ing.

O Lord, save Thy peo-ple, and bless Thine

heritage. Govern them and lift them up for ev - er.

Tempo primo.

Day by day we mag - ni -fy Thee; And we wor - ship Thy name, ev-er

f Tempo primo.

world without end. Vouchsafe, O Lord, to keep us this day

with - out sin. O Lord, have mer - cy up - on us, have

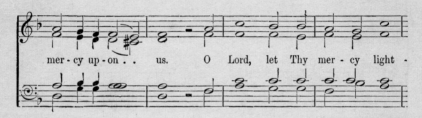

mer - cy up - on . . us. O Lord, let Thy mer - cy light -

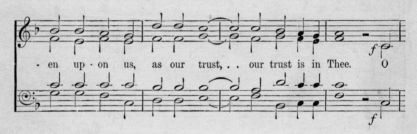

- en up - on us, as our trust, . . our trust is in Thee. O

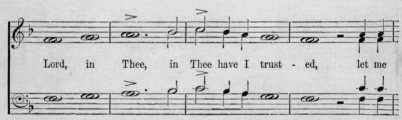

Lord, in Thee, in Thee have I trust - ed, let me

nev - er, let me nev - er be con - found - ed.

150   # We praise Thee, O God.

(TE DEUM LAUDAMUS.)

ALL THE VOICES IN UNISON.

J. STAINER.

Moderato, but to be sung Chant-wise, and not in strict time.

We praise Thee, O God, we acknowledge Thee to be the Lord. All the earth doth wor- ship Thee, the Fa - ther ev - er - last-ing. To Thee all angels cry a - loud, the heavens, and all the powers there- in. To Thee cheru - bin and ser - a - phin con - tin-ual-ly do cry,

This *Te Deum* may be sung in *Unison* throughout, the voices taking the upper part only.

Copyright, 1893, by Novello, Ewer and Co.

WE PRAISE THEE, O GOD.

HARMONY.

Slowly.

Ho-ly, ho-ly, ho-ly, Lord God of Sab-a-oth; Heaven and earth are full of the ma-jes-ty of Thy glo-ry. The glo-ri-ous com-pa-ny of the a-pos-tles praise.... Thee. The

goodly fellowship of the pro - phets praise . . . Thee. The

no - ble ar - my of mar - tyrs praise . . . Thee. The

ho - ly Church throughout all the world, doth ac - know - ledge

Thee; The Fa - ther of an in - fin-ite ma - jes - ty; Thine

cres.

hon - our-a - ble, true, and on - ly Son; Al - so the Ho - ly

pp *rall.* *a tempo.*

Ghost, the Com-fort - er. Thou art the King of Glo-ry, O . . . .

Christ. Thou art the ev-er-last-ing Son of . . the Fa - ther.

When Thou tookest up - on Thee to de - liv - er man, Thou didst not ab -

- hor the Vir - gin's womb. When Thou hadst ov - er - come the sharp-ness of

death, Thou didst o - pen the king-dom of heaven to all be - liev - ers.

mf Thou sittest at the right hand of God, in the Glo - ry of the

Fa - ther. We believe that Thou shalt come to .. be .. our ..

judge. We therefore pray Thee, help Thy servants, whom Thou hast re-deem-ed

with Thy precious blood. Make them to be num-ber-ed with Thy saints, in

glory ev-er-last-ing. O Lord, save Thy people, and bless Thine her-it -

- age.   Gov - ern   them   and   lift them up for   ev - er.

Day   by   day   we   mag-ni-fy   Thee ;   And we worship Thy name, ev - er

world with-out   end.   Vouch - safe, O Lord, to keep us this day with - out

151 We praise Thee, O God.

(TE DEUM LAUDAMUS.)

J. B. DYKES.

we acknowledge Thee to be .. the Lord.

We praise Thee, O God,

All the earth doth worship Thee, the Fa-ther ev-er-last-ing. To

Thee all an-gels cry a-loud, the heavens, and all the powers there-

- in. To Thee che-ru - bin and ser - a - phin con - tin - ual - ly do cry,

Ho - ly, ho - ly, ho - ly, . . Lord God of Sab - a - oth; Heaven

. . and earth are full of the ma - jes - ty of Thy glo - ry.

praise . . Thee.

The glo-rious com - pany of the a - pos - tles praise Thee.

praise . . Thee.

The goodly fel - lowship of . . the prophets praise Thee.

The no - ble ar - my of . . . mar - tyrs praise Thee. The

praise . . Thee.

ho - ly Church throughout all the world .. doth ac - knowledge Thee; The

Fa - ther of an in-finite ma - jesty: Thine honourable, true, and on-ly

Son; Al - so the Ho - ly Ghost, the Com - fort - er.

WE PRAISE THEE, O GOD.

Thou art the King of Glo-ry, O . . . . Christ. Thou art the ev-er-last-ing Son, the Son . . of the Fa-ther.

When Thou took-est up-on Thee to de-liv-er man, Thou

didst not ab-hor the Vir-gin's womb. When Thou hadst o-ver-come the sharp-ness of death, Thou didst o-pen the kingdom of hea-ven to all . . . be-liev-ers. Thou sit-test at the

WE PRAISE THEE, O GOD.

right .. hand of God, in the glo-ry of the Fa-ther.

We be-lieve that Thou shalt come to be . . . our judge.

We be-lieve that Thou shalt come . . to be our judge.

We be-lieve that Thou shalt come to be . . . our judge.

TENORS AND BASSES.

We there-fore pray Thee, help Thy ser-vants, whom Thou hast re-

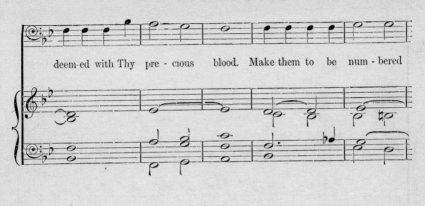

deem-ed with Thy pre - cious blood. Make them to be num - bered

with Thy saints, in glo - ry ev - er - last - - -

O Lord, save, . . save Thy peo - ple, and bless . .

· ing.

TENORS AND BASSES.

Vouchsafe, O Lord, to keep us, to keep us this day with-out .. sin. O Lord, have mer - cy up-on .. us, have mer - - - cy up - on us. O .. Lord, let Thy mer - cy light - en up-us.

152

We praise Thee, O God.

(TE DEUM LAUDAMUS.)

H. SMART.

We praise Thee, O God, we ac - knowledge Thee to be the Lord. All the earth doth worship Thee, the Father ev - er - last - ing. To Thee all an - gels cry a - loud, the heavens, and all the

(431)

powers therein. To Thee cherubin and ser - a - phin con - tin- ual - ly do

cry, . .   Ho - ly,
cry,   Ho - ly,   ho - ly,   ho -
cry, . .   Ho - ly,

Heaven . . . and earth are
- ly, Lord God of Sab - a - oth; Heaven and   earth are . .

full .. of the ma - jesty of Thy glo - ry.

The

praise . . . . Thee,

glorious com-pany of the a-pos-tles praise . . Thee, The

praise . . . . Thee. The

goodly fellowship of the prophets praise . . Thee.

(433)

WE PRAISE THEE, O GOD.

praise . . Thee.

no - ble ar - my of mar - tyrs praise . . . Thee. The

cres.

praise . . Thee. The

all the world doth acknowledge Thee;

- ho - ly Church throughout all the world doth ac-know - ledge Thee;
all the world doth acknowledge Thee; The

ho - ly Church throughout all the world doth ac - know - ledge Thee;

Thine hon - our - a - ble,

Fa - ther of an in - fin-ite maj - es - ty; Thine hon - our - a - ble,

Thine hon - our - a - ble,

dim.

true, and on - ly Son; Al - so the Ho - ly Ghost,

true, and on - ly Son; Al - so the Ho - ly Ghost, the

true, and on - ly Son; Al - so the Ho - ly Ghost,

Com - fort - er. Thou art the King of Glo - ry, O

Christ. Thou art the ev - er - last-ing Son of the Fa - ther.

ALL THE VOICES IN UNISON.

When Thou tookest up-on Thee to de-liv - - er man, Thou

didst not ab-hor the .. Vir-gin's womb. ..

When Thou hadst o-vercome the sharp - ness of death, Thou didst

o - pen the kingdom of heaven to all be-liev - ers. Thou

sit - test at the right hand of God, in the glo - ry of the

Fa - ther. We believe that Thou shalt come . . to be our

judge. . . We there-fore pray Thee, help Thy

ser - vants, whom Thou hast re - deem - ed . . with Thy precious

blood. . . Make . . them to be num - - bered
with Thy saints, in glo - - ry
ev - er - last - ing. O Lord, save Thy
peo - ple, and bless . . Thine her - it - age. Gov - ern

them and lift them up for ev - - er.

Day by day we . . mag-ni-fy . Thee; And we wor-ship Thy

name, ev - er world with-out . . end. Vouch-safe, O Lord, to keep us

this day without sin. O . . Lord, have mer-cy up-on us, have

mer-cy up-on us. O Lord, let Thy mer-cy light - en up-on us,

cres. *ritard.*

as our trust .. is in Thee. O Lord, in Thee, in

cres. *ritard.*

cres. *ritard.*

mf

Thee have I trusted, let .. me never be con - found - ed. . .

153 &lory be to &od on high.

(GLORIA IN EXCELSIS.)

All Voices in Unison.
Allegro moderato.

J. F. Bridge.

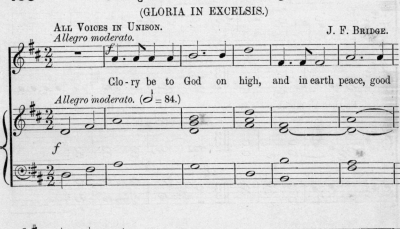

Clo - ry be to God on high, and in earth peace, good

Allegro moderato. ($\textbf{d} = 84$.)

will towards men. We praise Thee, we bless Thee, we wor - ship Thee, we

(441)

glo-ri-fy Thee,   we give thanks to Thee   for Thy great glo-

-ry,   O Lord God,   heaven-ly King,   God the

Fa-ther Al-might · y.   O Lord, the on-ly-begotten

Son Je - su Christ; O Lord God, Lamb of God, Son of   the Fa-ther, that

GLORY BE TO GOD ON HIGH.

Fa - ther, have mer - cy up - on us. For Thou on - ly art

ho - ly; Thou on - ly art the Lord; Thou

on - ly, O Christ, with the Ho - ly Ghost, art most high

in the glo - ry of God the Fa - ther. A - men.

Glory be to God on high.

(GLORIA IN EXCELSIS.)

J. NAYLOR.

P*

Fa - ther, have mer - cy up - on us. For Thou on - ly art

ho - ly; Thou on - ly art the Lord; Thou on - ly, O

Christ, with the Ho - ly Ghost, art most high in the

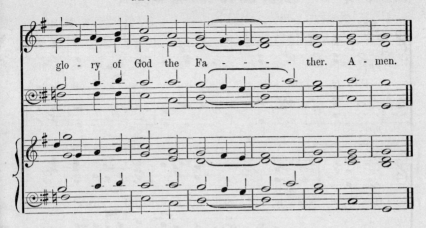

glo - ry of God the Fa - - - - ther. A - men.

155 ♯oly, ♯oly, ♯oly.

(SANCTUS.)

J. CAMIDGE.

Slowly.

Ho - ly, ho - ly, ho - ly, Lord God of hosts,

heaven and earth are full of Thy glo - ry: Glo - ry

be . . to Thee, O Lord . . . most . . high. A - men.

Holy, holy, holy.
(SANCTUS.)

W. H. Monk.

Ho - ly, ho - ly, ho - ly, Lord God . . of hosts,

Ho - ly, ho - ly, ho - ly, Lord God . . of hosts,

hea — ven and earth are full of Thy glo - - ry:

Glo - ry be to Thee, O

Lord . . . most high. A - men.

Holy, holy, holy.

(SANCTUS.)

T. Attwood.

Holy, holy, holy.

(SANCTUS.)

F. C. Maker.

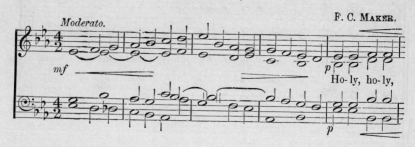

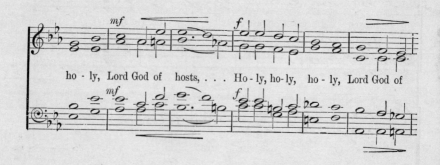

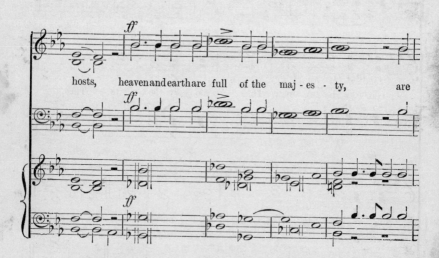

From *The Bristol Anthem Book*, by permission of Mr. W. Crotton Hemmons. Bristol.

full of the maj - es - ty of Thy glo - - ry:

Glo - ry be to Thee, O Lord most high, Glo - ry be to

Without organ.

Organ.

Thee, O Lord most high. A - - - men.

O Dayspring.

J. Stainer.

O Day-spring, O Day-spring! Brightness of the ev-er-last-ing Light, and Sun of Right-eous-ness; O Day-spring, O Day-spring Come, and en-light-en

them that sit in dark-ness, come, and en-light-en them that sit in

dark-ness.. and in the shadow of.. death, come, and en-light-en,

come, and en-light-en them that sit in dark-ness, come, come!

J. STAINER.

Moderato. (♩ = 60.)
Smoothly.

mf

cres.

Ped. ad lib.

O King, and De - sire of all na - tions, Thou

Cor - ner Stone, who hast made both one; Come, and save

form-edst from the clay,   come and save . .

man, come and save . . man.

Jesu, Word of God Incarnate.

C. Gounod.

Slowly.

Je - su, Word of God In - car - nate, Of the Vir - gin

mo - ther born; On the cross Thy sa - cred bod - y For us

men with nails was torn. Cleanse us in the sa - cred

cres. dim. p p

foun - tain, O - pened in . . Thy pierc - ed side; Feed us . .

cres. dim. p p

with Thy bod - y broken, Broken in death's ag - on - y.

O

O Jesu, hear us; O Jesu, save us: Je - su, Saviour,

Je - su, hear us ; O Je - su, save us:

hear our suppli - ca - tion. O grant us, Lord, Thy mer - cy, O grant us, Lord, Thy

mer - cy, O grant us, O grant us, Lord, Thy mer - cy. A -

A - men,

- men, A - men, A - men, A - men. . .

. . A - men . . A - men, . . A - men . .

Lord, for Thy tender mercies' sake.

R. Farrant.

LORD, FOR THY TENDER MERCIES' SAKE.

Abide with me.

H. F. Lyte.

R. G. Thompson.

With expression.

mf

A - bide with me: fast falls the ev - en - tide; The dark - ness
A - bide with me: fast falls .. the ev - en - tide;

mf

A - bide with me: fast falls the ev - en - tide;

cres.

deep - ens; Lord, with me a - bide: When other helpers fail, and

cres.

dim.

com - forts flee, Help of the helpless, O a - bide with me.

dim.

mf

Swift to its close .. ebbs out life's lit - tle day; Earth's joys grow
Swift to its close ebbs out ... life's lit - tle day;

mf

Swift to its close .. ebbs out life's lit - tle day;

From *The Bristol Anthem Book*, by permission of Mr. W. Crofton Hemmons Bristol

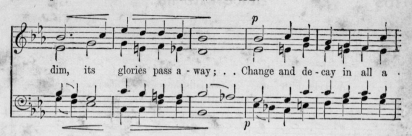

dim,   its   glories pass a - way ; . . Change and de - cay in all a

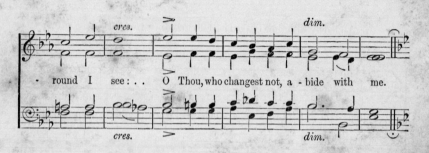

- round I   see : . .   O Thou, who changest not, a - bide with   me.

SOPRANOS ONLY. *Smoothly.*

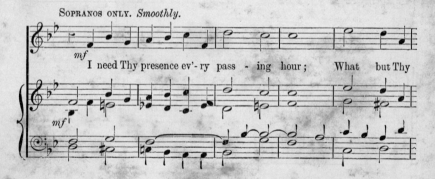

I need Thy presence ev'- ry pass - ing hour ;   What   but Thy

grace can foil the tempt - er's   power ? Who   like Thy - self my guide and

stay can be? Through cloud and sun-shine, O a-bide with me.

TENORS AND BASSES.

I fear no foe, with Thee at hand to bless;

Ills have no weight, and tears no bit-ter-ness:

ALL THE VOICES IN UNISON.

Where is death's sting? Where, grave, thy vic-to-ry? I

tri - umph still, if Thou a - bide with me.

HARMONY.

Hold Thou Thy cross be - fore my closing eyes, Shine through the gloom, and

point me to the skies; Heaven's morning breaks, and earth's vain shadows

Slower.

flee: In life and death, O Lord, a - bide with me. A - men.

Sun of my soul.

J. Keble.

E. Turner.

Andante con. moto. (♩ = 96.)

Sun of my soul, Thou Saviour dear, It is not night if Thou be near; O may no earth-born cloud a - rise To hide Thee from Thy servant's eyes. Sun of my soul, Thou Sav - iour dear,

It is not night if Thou be near.

Soprano Solo (or all the Sopranos).

When the soft dews of kind - ly sleep My wea - ried

Without Ped.

eye - lids gen - tly steep, Be my last thought, how

sweet to rest For ev - er on my Sa - viour's breast.

Be my last thought, how sweet to rest For ev - er, for

ev - er on my Sa - - viour's breast. *mf*

SOPRANO (OR BARITONE) SOLO, OR ALL THE SOPRANOS.

A - bide with me from morn till eve,

For without Thee I can - not live; A - bide with me when

night is nigh,   For with-out Thee I dare not die.

CHORUS.

A-bide with me when night is nigh, For with-out Thee I

dare not die. If some poor wan-d'ring child of Thine

Have spurned to-day the voice Di-vine, Now, Lord, the gra-cious

work be-gin; Let him no more lie down in sin.

TENORS AND BASSES.

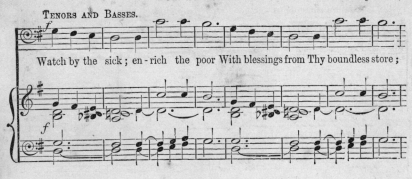

Watch by the sick; en - rich the poor With blessings from Thy boundless store;

CHORUS. *A little slower.*

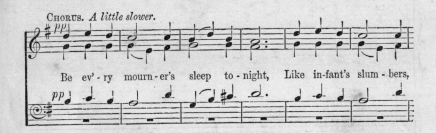

Be ev' - ry mourn - er's sleep to - night, Like in-fant's slum - bers,

pure and light. Be ev' - ry mourn - er's sleep to - night,

Like in - fant's slum - bers, pure . . . and light.

SUN OF MY SOUL.

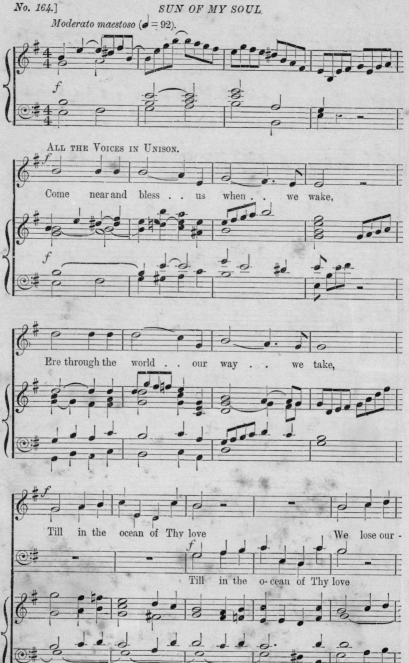

Moderato maestoso (= 92).

ALL THE VOICES IN UNISON.

Come near and bless . . us when . . we wake,

Ere through the world . . our way . . . we take,

Till in the ocean of Thy love We lose our -

Till in the o-cean of Thy love

- selves in heaven a - bove. Till in the o -cean of Thy

We lose our-selves in heaven a - bove. In the o-cean of Thy

love . . . . We lose our- selves in . . heaven, . . in

heaven . a - bove. . . . . .

165
The radiant morn.

G. THRING.

H. H. WOODWARD.

(475)

THE RADIANT MORN.

day, Its glo - rious noon, its noon how quickly past! Lead

us, O . . Christ, Thou liv - - ing Way, . . Safe

Lead us, O Christ, Thou living Way, . .

home . . at last,

home, safe home at last,   Lead us, O Christ, Thou
home   at   last,

Safe home at last,   safe home   at last,

166   # Lord, keep us safe this night.

(VESPER HYMN.)

Adapted from Beethoven.
Harmonised by J. E. West.

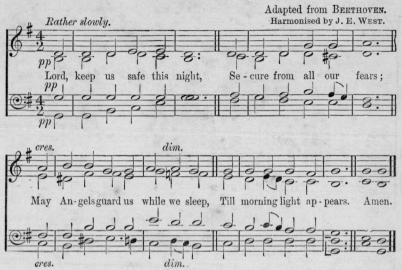

Lord, keep us safe this night, Se-cure from all our fears;

May An-gels guard us while we sleep, Till morning light ap-pears. Amen.

167   # Lord, keep us safe this night.

(VESPER HYMN.)

B. Steane.

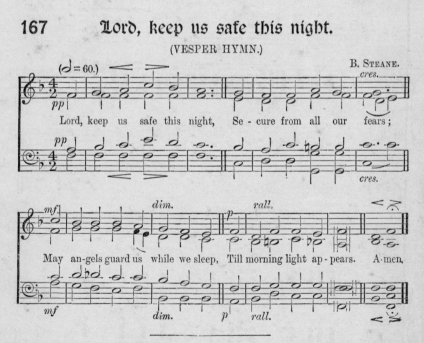

Lord, keep us safe this night, Se-cure from all our fears;

May an-gels guard us while we sleep, Till morning light ap-pears. A-men.